OCS Study
MMS 2004-071

Data Quality Control and Emissions Inventories of OCS Oil and Gas Production Activities in the Breton Area of the Gulf of Mexico

Final Report

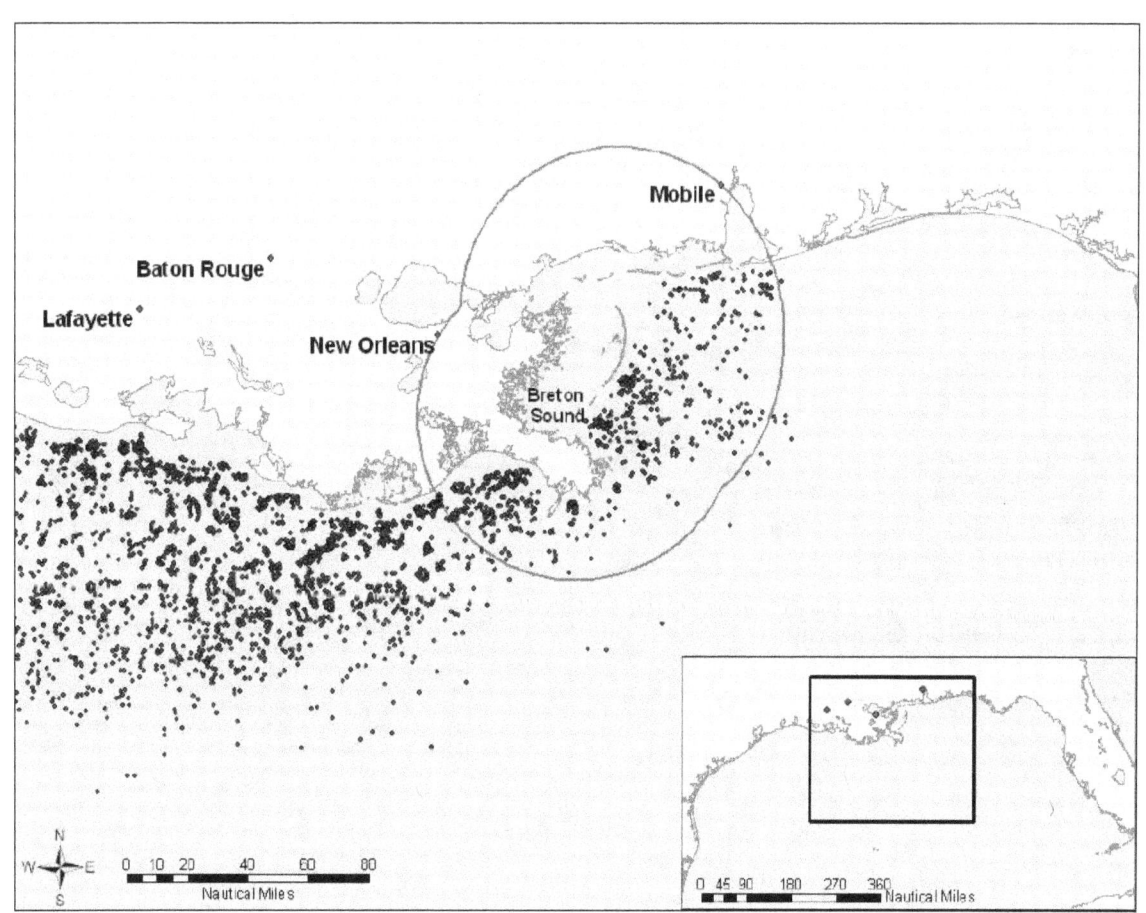

MMS U.S. Department of the Interior
Minerals Management Service
Gulf of Mexico OCS Region

OCS Study
MMS 2004-071

Data Quality Control and Emissions Inventories of OCS Oil and Gas Production Activities in the Breton Area of the Gulf of Mexico

Final Report

Authors

Richard Billings
Darcy Wilson
Eastern Research Group, Inc.
Morrisville, North Carolina

Prepared under MMS Contract
1435-01-01-CT-31163
by
Eastern Research Group, Inc.
1600 Perimeter Park Drive
Morrisville, North Carolina 27560

Published by

U.S. Department of the Interior
Minerals Management Service
Gulf of Mexico OCS Region

New Orleans
October 2004

DISCLAIMER

This report was prepared under contract between the Minerals Management Service (MMS) and Eastern Research Group, Inc. This report has been technically reviewed by the MMS and approved for publication. Approval does not signify that the contents necessarily reflect the views and policies of the MMS, nor does mention of trade names or commercial products constitute endorsement or recommendation for use. It is, however, exempt from review and compliance with the MMS editorial standards.

REPORT AVAILABILITY

Extra copies of this report may be obtained from the Public Information Office (Mail Stop 5034) at the following address:

U.S. Department of the Interior
Minerals Management Service
Gulf of Mexico OCS Region
Public Information Office (MS 5034)
1201 Elmwood Park Boulevard
New Orleans, Louisiana 70123-2394

Telephone: (504) 736-2519 or
              1-800-200-GULF

CITATION

Suggested citation:

Billings, R.S. and D.L. Wilson. 2004. Data Quality Control and Emissions Inventories of OCS Oil and Gas Production Activities in the Breton Area of the Gulf of Mexico: Final Report. U.S. Dept. of the Interior, Minerals Management Service, Gulf of Mexico OCS Region, New Orleans, LA. OCS Study MMS 2004-071. 94 pp.

ACKNOWLEDGMENTS

This report would not have been possible without the contributions of the following staff at ERG, Inc.: Roger Chang, Andy Blackard, Regi Oommen, Heather Perez, Melodie Vines, and Jody Tisano. Invaluable assistance was also provided by the staff of COMM Engineering, Inc., particularly Brian Boyer and Christy Chadick.

TABLE OF CONTENTS

TABLE OF CONTENTS (CONTINUED)

LIST OF FIGURES

LIST OF TABLES

LIST OF TABLES (CONTINUED)

1. EXECUTIVE SUMMARY

The Minerals Management Service (MMS) is responsible for assessing the potential impacts of air pollutant emissions from offshore oil and gas exploration, development, and production sources in the Outer Continental Shelf (OCS). This responsibility is driven by the OCS Lands Act, which directs MMS to regulate OCS emission sources to assure that they do not significantly affect onshore air quality. The MMS air quality regulations are contained in 30 CFR 250.302 through 304. In particular, MMS must assess the impact of emissions from platform and other OCS sources on the air quality of the Breton National Wildlife Refuge/Wilderness Area (BNWA), a Prevention of Significant Deterioration Class I Area. Under the Clean Air Act, air quality degradation is to be limited in Class I areas. To assess the emissions of offshore oil and gas platforms and their associated emissions, the MMS conducted some limited emission inventories in the Gulf of Mexico in the 1980s. In 1991, the MMS sponsored a regional ozone modeling effort conducted by the U.S. Environmental Protection Agency (EPA) using the Regional Oxidant Modeling (ROM). The Gulf of Mexico Air Quality Study was initiated that same year, and activity data for a Gulfwide emission inventory were collected for a one-year period in 1991-1992.

The MMS' Gulf of Mexico OCS Regional office sponsored this project, *the Data Quality Control and Emissions Inventories of OCS Oil and Gas Production Activities in the Breton Area of the Gulf of Mexico* (MMS Contract No. 1435-01-01-CT-31163). The MMS' Gulf of Mexico OCS Regional office also sponsored two similar projects, the *Gulfwide Emission Inventory for the Regional Haze and Ozone Modeling Effort* Study (MMS Contract No. 00-01-CT-31021) (Wilson et al. 2004), and the *Emission Inventories of OCS Production and Development Activities in the Gulf of Mexico* (MMS Contract No. 1435-01-98-CT-30856) (Coe et al. 2003). This study builds upon these studies with the goal of developing an air pollution emissions inventory, for the period from September 2000 through August 2001, for all OCS oil and gas production-related sources within 100 kilometers (km) of the BNWA, including non-platform sources. Pollutants covered in this inventory are nitrogen oxides (NO_x) and sulfur dioxide (SO_2).

To develop the inventory, the Breton Offshore Activities Data System (BOADS) was created, which was used to collect monthly activity data from platform sources. The activity data were combined with the most recent emission factors published by the EPA and Emission Inventory Improvement Program (EIIP) emission estimation methods to develop a comprehensive emissions inventory for NO_x and SO_2. Non-platform emission estimates were developed for sources such as commercial marine vessels and helicopters. MMS will use the results of this study to determine how NO_x and SO_2 concentrations have changed over time in the BNWA.

2. INTRODUCTION

2.1 BACKGROUND

The Breton National Wilderness Area (BNWA), part of the Breton National Wildlife Refuge, is classified as a Class I area under the U.S. Environmental Protection Agency's (EPA's) Prevention of Significant Deterioration (PSD) regulations. The BNWA is managed by the U.S. Fish and Wildlife Service. Under the Clean Air Act, air quality degradation is limited in Class I areas by establishing stringent "increment" limits for nitrogen oxides (NO_x) and sulfur dioxide (SO_2). These increments are the maximum increases in ambient pollutant concentrations allowed over baseline concentrations. The Minerals Management Service (MMS) is responsible for determining if air pollutant concentrations of NO_x and SO_2 have changed over time in the Gulf of Mexico in the vicinity of the BNWA due to emissions from oil and natural gas production sources.

In response to this mandate, MMS has developed an overall strategy to deal with Outer Continental Shelf (OCS) oil and gas production activities that could affect the BNWA. This includes developing inventories of platform emissions, conducting air quality monitoring activities, and establishing a review process for new plans that includes close coordination with the Fish and Wildlife Service.

Currently there are three studies which will provide the MMS with databases describing the OCS oil and gas production emissions during four periods. The periods cover all of the years 1977, 1988, and 2000; and this study, which covers 12 consecutive months from September 1, 2000 to August 31, 2001.

2.2 SCOPE AND PURPOSE OF THIS PROJECT

The inventory study period covered in this report, 12 consecutive months from September 1, 2000 to August 31, 2001, coincides with air quality monitoring activities in the Breton area. Through an Office of Management and Budget-approved Information Collection Request, MMS required affected platform operators to collect and submit the activity data needed to develop emission estimates for NO_x and SO_2 from platform activities. Affected operators are lessees and operators of federal oil, gas, and sulphur leases within 100 kilometers (km) of the BNWA. MMS published Notice to Lessees and Operators (NTL) 99-G14 to inform operators about the Breton Area study, and an August 16, 1999 meeting they were to attend to learn more about the activity data request and their role.

MMS developed and distributed a Visual Basic program for platform operators to use to collect and submit activity data on a monthly basis. The program, known as the Breton Offshore Activities Data System (BOADS), was used by operators to submit activity data for a number of production platform emission sources. Operators used the BOADS software to collect activity data for amine units, boilers/heaters/burners, diesel engines, drilling equipment, flares, and natural gas engines and turbines.

These activity data were used to calculate SO_2 and NO_x emissions. The Breton Oracle database management system (DBMS) calculates and archives the activity data and the resulting emissions estimates. Database users can query by pollutant, month, equipment type, platform, etc.

2.3 STUDY OBJECTIVES

The objectives of this study are to use the BOADS Visual Basic data collection software (written in Access) to collect activity data from platform sources located within 100 km of the BNWA, quality control (QC) the activity data, use the activity data to develop monthly emission estimates of NO_x and SO_2, and develop NO_x and SO_2 emission estimates for non-platform sources within 100 km of the BNWA. Sources within 100 km the BNWA were targeted because MMS is responsible for determining if air pollutant concentrations of NO_x and SO_2 have changed over time in the vicinity of the BNWA. MMS' Oracle DBMS was updated and used to calculate and archive platform emissions estimates using the most current emission factors, calculation methods, and activity data.

2.4 REPORT ORGANIZATION

Following this introduction, the *Data Quality Control and Emissions Inventories of OCS Platform Activities in the Breton Area of the Gulf of Mexico* report is organized as follows:

- Section 3 discusses how the platform activity data were collected and compiled for sources near the BNWA.

- Section 4 summarizes the quality assurance/quality control procedures that were implemented after receipt of the files to prepare the data for use in developing emission calculations. The approach used to fill in data gaps in the platform data is also discussed in Section 4.

- Calculation methods for each piece of platform equipment are presented in Section 5. These calculation routines are performed in the Oracle DBMS.

- Calculation methods for non-platform sources are discussed in Section 6.

- Section 7 summarizes the resulting emission estimates by equipment type and pollutant. The limitations associated with the data and the emission estimates are also noted in Section 7.

- References cited throughout the report are listed in Section 8.

-

3. DATA COLLECTION

3.1 INTRODUCTION

To develop the NO_x and SO_2 inventory for all oil and gas platforms within 100 km of the BNWA, MMS collected activity data from platform operators from September 2000 through August 2001. The objective was to collect, perform QC, and archive activity data from platform sources near the BNWA that emit SO_2 and NO_x.

This section of the report outlines the steps taken to collect the data, including meeting with and training platform operators, and answering questions about data collection. The activity data collected were used to calculate emission estimates using the most current emission factors and calculation methods.

3.2 SOFTWARE DISTRIBUTION

A workshop was held in New Orleans on August 16, 1999 to discuss and explain the information collection and reporting procedures, the pollutants to be covered, and the reasons the Breton study was undertaken. MMS introduced the BOADS Visual Basic activity data collection program at the workshop, and allowed users to install and use the software firsthand. MMS walked operators through installing the software, entering data, and reporting data.

The *User's Guide for the Breton Offshore Activities Data System (BOADS) for Air Quality* (Coe et al. 2001) was the primary source of information for operators. The guide was made available to all users on the MMS Gulf of Mexico Region web site, where it could be downloaded and printed. The guide contains instructions on installation, starting and exiting BOADS, creating and editing data, quality control, and saving and backing up files.

MMS had an initial test period of the BOADS software for September and October, 1999. The test period was designed to allow operators to enter limited activity data and gain familiarity with the software and data entry requirements. The test period also allowed MMS to evaluate the functionality of the program and problems encountered by the users.

3.3 OPERATOR USE OF BOADS SOFTWARE TO COMPILE DATA

Once operators attended the training workshop, obtained the software, and participated in the test period, they were ready to begin entering and submitting activity data on a monthly basis. The initial data collection phase was to run from January 2000 through December 2000. The collection phase was then extended through August 2001.

MMS communicated with operators through the MMS web site using Frequently Asked Questions (FAQs) posted on their web site, and via email and telephone. The designated support staff were Mr. Joe Perryman and Mr. YP Desai.

For each emission source, there is an equipment screen that contains fields for the parameters to be recorded. As an example, the boiler/heater/burner equipment screens require operators to enter parameters such as hours operated, fuel type, fuel heating value, amount of fuel used, and equipment elevation. For details on equipment parameters, see Appendix A of the *User's Guide for the Breton Offshore Activities Data System for Air Quality* (Coe et al. 2001).

3.4   QUALITY CONTROL CHECKS

Quality control procedures were programmed into the software in an effort to minimize the submittal of incomplete and erroneous activity data by the platform operators. The software automatically runs a series of QC checks on the data when the operator saves it. If the operator leaves a field blank, provides data that are out of range, or enters a value that is not consistent on a month-to-month basis, an error message will appear. The operator can either: correct the problem, override the QC check (and provide a comment), or ignore the message and save the file anyway. When operators entered data that appeared in the QC results, ERG attempted to reconcile the missing, atypical, or suspect data by reviewing the comments, contacting the operators, or developing surrogate data as described in Section 4 of this report.

4. QUALITY ASSURANCE/QUALITY CONTROL

4.1   INTRODUCTION

Platform operators submitted data files generated by the BOADS software. Fifty-five companies submitted data for 599 active or inactive platforms (combination of complex ID and structure ID). Included in the submittal were 631 survey records and 6,950 structure records. A unique survey record is a combination of user ID and month. A unique structure record is a combination of complex ID, structure ID, and month.

This section summarizes the data received, the steps ERG took to review the monthly BOADS data for completeness and accuracy, and the types of errors encountered. Also discussed in this section are the procedures used to correct and gap-fill missing data. When operators failed to enter data or entered data that were atypical or suspect, ERG attempted to reconcile the data by reviewing the comments, contacting the operators, or developing surrogate data.

Prior to performing the quality checks noted below, the submitted data were evaluated to identify any extraneous data that should be removed. For example, 97 platforms only submitted the structures table; no equipment tables were provided. These platforms were removed from the data set. For 87 platforms, data were provided only for fugitive emission sources, and one platform submitted data only for a glycol dehydrator and storage tanks. As volatile organic compound (VOC) sources are not included in this inventory, these 88 platforms were removed from the dataset. 30 platforms reported that they were inactive for the whole 12 month period that the inventory covers. These 30 platforms were also removed, leaving 384 active platforms in the BNWA inventory.

4.2   USER, STRUCTURE, AND COMPLEX IDS

The BOADS files that were submitted were appended into one composite database. QC checks were performed on the composite database to insure that the user ID, complex ID, structure ID, area, block, structure name, longitude, latitude, and lease numbers were correct in the structure table.

Approximately 47% of the 384 platforms completed all 12 surveys. The remaining 203 platforms submitted between 1 and 11 surveys. For 18 platforms it was clear that there was a change of ownership – with months submitted under two different user IDs. MMS staff contacted the other platform operators to obtain data for the months where data submittals were not made.

There were 2 companies that reported data for the months January through August of 2000, but these months are not included in the inventory time period. These submittals accounted for 776 records in the structure table and were removed from the activity database.

MMS' field officers contacted the platform operators who submitted data that were missing months. The platform operators provided data for 25 platforms. Most of the supplemental files provided were still missing monthly records.

For the remaining platforms with missing monthly data, surrogate data were developed depending upon the amount of platform specific data that were provided. When a platform operator submitted three or more months of data, averages of the submitted platform data were used to fill the data gaps for the missing months. When a platform provided only one or two months, Gulfwide averages were developed from the Gulfwide Inventory dataset (Wilson et al. 2004) and used to fill the data gaps from the missing months.

4.2.1 Platforms

The first quality check performed on the submitted data was on the user, complex, and structure IDs. This check was implemented by comparing the submitted IDs to the master list obtained from the MMS web page, and the IDs used in the Gulfwide Inventory database. After reformatting the IDs, 379 out of the 599 platforms were matched to platforms on master list. Of the remaining 220 platforms, 16 matched platforms in the Gulfwide Inventory database.

The remaining 204 platforms that did not match either database were manually matched by comparing the complex and structure IDs. Using these two fields, 113 platforms were matched to those on the master list or the Gulfwide Inventory database. The remaining 91 platforms were manually matched by comparing the area, block, and structure IDs. Once the platforms were matched, the complex or structure ID were corrected to match the ID in the master list.

There were 3 platforms that could not be identified with the information given in the structure table. One of these platforms, SL 13718, was removed from the inventory because it was determined to be in state waters and not part of the scope of the BNWA Inventory project. There are only two platforms that could not be identified.

4.2.2 User ID

A wide range of problems were encountered during checks of the user IDs. Many of the problems related to changes in ownership. In order to handle user ID problems consistently, a generic list was developed of the types of problems encountered and the required actions to be taken to revise the user IDs.

Thirty-three percent of the user IDs submitted needed to be corrected. For example, some companies put their name in this field, not their user ID number; these mistakes were corrected as they were identified.

There were several companies that used the ID *sail*. These records could not be appended into the user and the survey tables, as these were flagged as duplicates because the user ID is the primary key for both of these tables. The *sail* user ID was associated with four user IDs. For one of the companies, the user ID was corrected based on the master list. Range Resources was not on the master list; the user ID for HR Resources was used as they were noted to be the owner of the platform based on the platform ID and lease number. Of the remaining two companies, Basin Exploration, Inc. merged with Stone Energy Corporation, so the user ID for Stone Energy was applied to both. Exxon and Mobil used the same ID (00276) included in the master list. For the Gulfwide Inventory, their data were submitted together, so this did not pose a problem in incorporating the data into the database. But in this study, the data were submitted separately and were flagged as duplicates and therefore could not be easily appended into the survey and user tables. Considering they used the same IDs in the Gulfwide Inventory and none of the platforms were truly duplicates, their submittals were manually merged and the name and user ID included in MMS' master list was applied to their data.

4.2.3 Area

Necessary corrections to the area field were made where errors were encountered. Some companies gave the appropriate abbreviation for this field, while other companies used the full text name of the area. In this QC check, the correct abbreviations were used where non-abbreviated data were submitted.

4.2.4 Block

The block field was also checked to insure that the submitted data matched the MMS database. Most of the block records were correct, but some companies included extraneous information in the block field, and a few companies used the structure name in the block field rather than the block code. Where necessary, records were changed to match the MMS database.

4.2.5 Structure Name

In the structure name field, many companies populated this field incorrectly. Those platforms that matched either the MMS master list or the final Gulfwide Inventory database were not changed. Those platforms that did not match either were updated to match the MMS master or Gulfwide Inventory lists. Many of the changes that needed to be made were minor corrections.

4.2.6 Latitude/Longitude Coordinates

Latitude and longitude coordinates of the platforms were checked. Most of the coordinates were correct, but some of the submitted coordinates differed from the coordinates in the MMS master list. These data were replaced with the coordinates in the MMS master list. For those platforms that were in the Gulfwide Inventory database and not on the master table, the coordinates were revised using the coordinates in the Gulfwide Inventory database. The two platforms that were not matched to either list retained their coordinates.

4.2.7 Lease Numbers

Many companies reported their lease number using different formats. To make all lease numbers consistent, the following format was used: OCS-G-XXXXX, where the X's represent the 5 digit lease number.

The lease ID numbers were compared to the MMS master table. Only two lease numbers needed to be changed. Because ownership changes frequently, it is often difficult to identify who owns the platform currently and who owned it when the data were collected. The two lease numbers that did change were obviously wrong and they were updated to the lease numbers provided in the MMS master list.

4.3   EQUIPMENT SUMMARIES

The platform operators provided monthly, process-specific data. These data are used in the emission estimating procedures discussed in Section 5 of this report to estimate monthly and annual emissions. To insure that the equipment data were complete and reasonable, a variety of quality checks were performed.

Table 4-1 summarizes the completeness review of specified equipment. Where possible, surrogate stack parameter data were used based on knowledge of platform operations and equipment to fill the identified data gaps. These surrogate stack parameter values are noted in Table 4-2. Surrogate values were calculated for exit velocity from the submitted data. Other surrogate data were developed from Gulfwide industry averages. It should be noted that surrogate stack parameters were not needed for all equipment; only the surrogates that were needed are shown in Table 4-2. For stack elevation, the BOADS program requested different values for flares that for other equipment. For flares, the program requested that operators enter stack outlet elevation (above mean sea level). For all other equipment, the program requested that operators enter equipment elevation and outlet height (above the equipment).

Table 4-1. Equipment Completeness Summary.

Equipment Table	Number of Units	Total Active Monthly Submittals Received	Total Possible Active Monthly Submittals[a]	Completeness
Amine Units	6	48	58	0.8276
Boilers	170	1480	1646	0.8991
Diesel Engines	831	7333	8269	0.8868
Drilling Equipment	103	247	N/A[b]	N/A
Flares	57	466	555	0.8396
Glycol Dehydrators	141	1337	1499	0.8919
Natural Gas Engines	578	5532	5964	0.9276
Natural Gas Turbines	158	1538	1689	0.9106

[a] Total possible submittals include adjustments to account for months when the equipment is flagged as inactive
[b] Not applicable; drilling operations are intermittent making it impossible to estimate possible submittals

Table 4-2. Surrogate Stack Parameters Used to Supplement BOADS Data.

Unit	Field	Default Value
Boiler/heater/burner	Max rated fuel use (natural gas)	1,604 scf/hr
Boiler/heater/burner	Avg. fuel use (natural gas)	980 scf/hr
Diesel Engine	Max rated fuel use	7,049 Btu/hp-hr
Diesel Engine	Avg. fuel use	5,893 Btu/hp-hr
Diesel Engine– exhaust system	Exit temperature	739 °F
Flare	Exit temperature	1,215 °F
Flare	Outlet diameter	13 inches
Flare	Stack outlet elevation	186 ft above sea level
Natural Gas Engine	Max rated fuel use	7,000 Btu/hp-hr
Natural Gas Engine	Avg. fuel use	7,000 Btu/hp-hr
Natural Gas Engine– exhaust system	Exit temperature	1,100 °F
Natural Gas Turbine	Max rated fuel use	10,458 Btu/hp-hr
Natural Gas Turbine	Avg. fuel use	9,668 Btu/hp-hr
Natural Gas Turbine– exhaust system	Exit temperature	878 °F
Natural Gas Turbine– exhaust system	Outlet height	33 feet above unit

The completeness of the submitted data needed to calculate emissions is discussed below for each of the equipment types included in this inventory. Special attention was paid to data elements that are required to calculate emissions (not stack parameters) because the goal of developing this inventory was to develop emission estimates for all active emission sources on a monthly basis. Thus, missing data elements such as amount of fuel used and hours operated needed to be populated if the equipment were considered active (operating) for any given month. In these cases, the missing data were populated with platform specific or Gulfwide Inventory averages. When a platform operator submitted three or more months of data, averages of the submitted platform data were used to fill the data gaps for the missing months. When a platform provided only one or two months, Gulfwide averages were developed from the Gulfwide Inventory dataset (Wilson et al, 2004) and used to fill the data gaps from the missing months.

4.3.1 Amine Units

The amine unit table was only populated by four companies with a total of six units. One of these units was flagged as inactive. Of the five remaining amine units, two had sulfur recovery. The remaining three amine units flared their emissions to the atmosphere.

4.3.2 Boilers/Heaters/Burners

There are 170 boilers operating on 112 platforms for 44 companies. The completeness range of the submitted data for required fields for which surrogates could not be developed was between 97 to 99%.

4.3.3 Diesel Engines

Fifty one companies operate 831 diesel engines on 380 platforms in the Breton Area. Completeness for required fields for which surrogates could not be developed was between 99 and 100%.

4.3.4 Drilling Rigs

One hundred and three drilling rigs operate on 65 platforms for 10 different companies. Completeness for required fields for which surrogates could not be readily developed ranged from 82 to 100%.

4.3.5 Flares

Nineteen companies operate 57 flares on 48 platforms. For required fields that surrogates could not be readily developed completeness ranged from 94 to 100%.

For occasional flare operations, 11 companies reported that there were 24 flare occurrences on 24 platforms. The completeness for required fields was good, ranging from 99 to 100%.

4.3.6 Natural Gas Engines

Fifty three companies operate 578 natural gas engines on 244 platforms. One hundred percent of the submittals were provided with complete data for all fields.

4.3.7 Natural Gas Turbines

There are 158 natural gas turbines operating on 67 platforms for 21 companies in the Breton Area. One hundred percent of the submittals were complete.

4.4 FUEL USAGE SUMMARIES

Boilers/heaters/burners, diesel and natural gas reciprocating engines, and natural gas turbines are all very important emission sources on a platform. Fuel usage data were requested at the structure level, as well as for individual pieces of equipment. To verify that emissions are not overestimated for the individual combustion sources, multiple data elements were reviewed and corrections made based on direction provided by MMS staff:

- Where hours of operation for a given month were larger than the number of hours in the month, the maximum possible hours replaced the submitted hours.

- Where operating horsepower was larger than maximum rated horsepower, the maximum horsepower value replaced the reported operating horsepower.

- The reported fuel usage for individual equipment was evaluated to insure that fuel usage was not larger than the theoretical maximum fuel usage.

- The sum of fuel used for each piece of equipment located on a platform was compared to the total fuel used for the structure.

4.4.1 Boilers/Heaters/Burners

The submitted boiler/heater/burner data were checked to insure that the following gaseous fuel usage conditions were consistent:

$$\text{Maximum Fuel Usage Rate (scf / hr)} = \frac{\text{Maximum Rated Heat Input } (10^6 \text{ Btu / hr})}{\text{Fuel Heating Value (Btu / scf)}}$$

$$\text{Average Fuel Usage Rate (scf / hr)} = \frac{\text{Average Heat Input } (10^6 \text{ Btu / hr})}{\text{Fuel Heating Value (Btu / scf)}}$$

The boiler/heater/burner data were also checked to insure that the following liquid fuel usage conditions were consistent:

$$\text{Maximum Fuel Usage Rate (lb / hr)} = \frac{\text{Maximum Rated Heat Input } (10^6 \text{ Btu / hr})}{\text{Fuel Heating Value (Btu / hr)}}$$

$$\text{Average Fuel Usage Rate (lb / hr)} = \frac{\text{Average Heat Input } (10^6 \text{ Btu / hr})}{\text{Fuel Heating Value (But / lb)}}$$

Approximately 30% of active boilers had at least one month where the calculated and reported maximum fuel usage differed by at least 15%. Fifty-four percent of active boilers had at least one month where the calculated and reported average fuel usage rate differed by at least 15%. Where the average fuel usage rate was greater than the maximum rated fuel usage, the maximum fuel usage rate replaced the average fuel usage rate as noted in the following flow diagram:

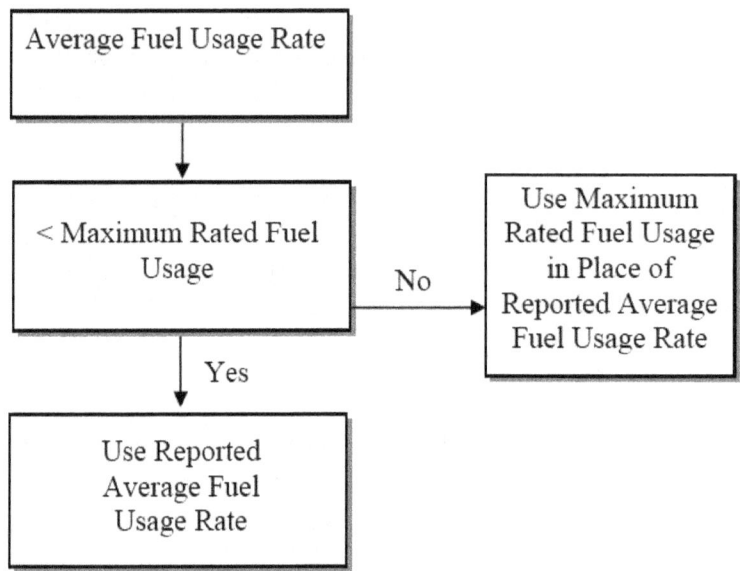

Total fuel use at the equipment level was also evaluated to insure that the total fuel use data were consistent with fuel usage at maximum horsepower and the hours of operation. Where the total fuel use was greater than the calculated fuel use at maximum horsepower, the maximum fuel use replaced the total fuel use as illustrated in the following flow chart:

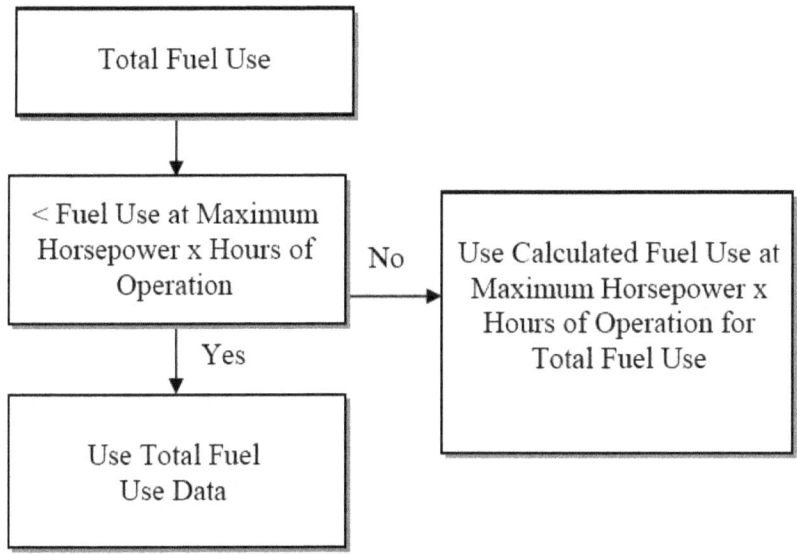

4.4.2 Diesel Engines

The submitted diesel engine data were initially checked to insure that the maximum rated and average fuel usage was reasonable. For diesel engines with a maximum horsepower rating equal to or greater than 300 horsepower, if the maximum rated fuel usage rate or average fuel usage was less than 6,300 Btu/hp-hr or greater than 7,700 Btu/hp-hr, the fuel usage was changed to 7,000 Btu/hp-hr. This correction needed to be made for 19% of the diesel engine records. The fuel usage rate for engines with maximum horsepower less than 300 horsepower can legitimately be greater than 7,700 Btu/hp-hr or less than 6,300 Btu/hp-hr, therefore the fuel usage values for these engines were not corrected.

Where the maximum rated or average fuel usage was changed, the fuel used at maximum horsepower and total fuel used were also changed as noted in the equations below:

$$\text{Fuel Used at Maximum Horsepower (gal)} = \frac{(\text{Max Horsepower}) \times (7,000 \text{ Btu}/\text{hp-hr}) \times (\text{Hrs of Operation})}{(\text{Fuel Heating Value (Btu}/\text{lb})) \times (7.1 \text{ lbs}/\text{gal})}$$

$$\text{Total Fuel Used (gal)} = \frac{(\text{Operating Horsepower}) \times (7,000 \text{ Btu}/\text{hp-hr}) \times (\text{Hrs of Operation})}{(\text{Fuel Heating Value (Btu}/\text{lb})) \times (7.1 \text{ lbs}/\text{gal})}$$

All diesel engine data were checked to ensure that total fuel used at the equipment level was consistent with fuel used at maximum horsepower. For 4% of diesel engines, the total fuel used was greater than fuel used at maximum horsepower. For these cases the data were adjusted based on the approach noted above for boilers, heaters, and burners.

4.4.3 Natural Gas Reciprocating Engines

The submitted natural gas engine data were initially checked to insure that the maximum rated and average fuel usage were reasonable. For natural gas engines that had a rating equal to or greater than 250 horsepower, if the maximum rated or average fuel usage was less than 6,300 Btu/hp-hr or greater than 7,700 Btu/hp-hr, then the fuel usage was changed to 7,000 Btu/hp-hr. This correction was made to 19% of the maximum rated fuel usage and 17% of the average fuel usage records. The fuel usage rate for engines with a maximum horsepower less than 250 horsepower can legitimately be greater than 7,700 Btu/hp-hr or less than 6,300 Btu/hp-hr, therefore the fuel usage for these engines were not corrected.

Where the fuel usage was changed, fuel used at maximum horsepower and total fuel used at the equipment level were corrected as noted in the equations below:

$$\text{Fuel Used at Maximum Horsepower (Mscf)} = \frac{(\text{Max Horsepower}) \times (7,000 \text{ Btu}/\text{hp-hr}) \times (\text{Hrs of Operation})}{(\text{Fuel Heating Value)} (\text{Btu}/\text{scf})) \times (1,000 \text{ scf}/\text{Mscf})}$$

$$\text{Total Fuel Used (Mscf)} = \frac{(\text{Operating Horsepower}) \times (7,000 \text{ Btu} / \text{hp-hr}) \times (\text{Hrs of Operation})}{(\text{Fuel Heating Value (Btu} / \text{scf)}) \times (1,000 \text{ scf} / \text{Mscf})}$$

All natural gas engine data were checked to insure that the total fuel used at the equipment level was consistent with the fuel used at maximum horsepower. For 11% of natural gas engine records, the total fuel used was greater than fuel used at maximum horsepower. For these cases the data were adjusted based on the approach noted above for boilers, heaters, and burners.

4.4.4 Natural Gas Turbines

The submitted natural gas turbine data were initially checked to insure that the fuel usage was reasonable. For active natural gas turbines, if the maximum rated or average fuel usage was less than 9,000 Btu/hp-hr or greater than 11,000 Btu/hp-hr, then the fuel usage was changed to 10,000 Btu/hp-hr. This correction needed to be made for 30% of maximum rated fuel usage records and 37% of average fuel usage records.

Where the fuel usage was corrected the fuel used at maximum horsepower and total fuel used at the equipment level was calculated as noted in the equations below:

$$\text{Fuel Used at Maximum Horsepower (Mscf)} = \frac{(\text{Max Horsepower}) \times (10,000 \text{ Btu} / \text{hp-hr}) \times (\text{Hrs of Operation})}{(\text{Fuel Heating Value (Btu} / \text{scf)}) \times (1,000 \text{ scf} / \text{Mscf})}$$

$$\text{Total Fuel Used (Mscf)} = \frac{(\text{Operating Horsepower}) \times (10,000 \text{ Btu} / \text{hp-hr}) \times (\text{Hrs of Operation})}{(\text{Fuel Heating Value (Btu} / \text{scf)}) \times (1,000 \text{ scf} / \text{Mscf})}$$

All active natural gas turbine data were checked to ensure that the total fuel use was consistent with the fuel use at maximum horsepower. For 4% of natural gas turbine records, the total fuel use was greater than fuel used at maximum horsepower. For these cases the data were adjusted based on the approach noted above for boilers, heaters, and burners.

4.4.5 Equipment Sum Fuel Usage Greater than Platform Total Fuel Usage

After the equipment fuel usage data were corrected, 103 platform surveys (approximately 19% of the submitted data) were identified where the sum of the diesel fuel usage for the individual diesel equipment associated with the platform was greater than the reported platform total diesel fuel usage. The platform total fuel usage was corrected in these cases to be equal to the total fuel usage of the individual equipment.

For 68 platform surveys (approximately 13% of the submitted data), the sum of the natural gas fuel usage for individual equipment operating on the platform was greater than the platform total natural gas fuel usage. The platform total fuel usage was corrected in these cases to be equal to the total fuel usage of the individual equipment.

4.5 OTHER QUALITY CHECKS THAT WERE PERFORMED ON THE SUBMITTED BOADS DATA

4.5.1 Active/Inactive Check

Operators had the opportunity to identify a platform as being either active or inactive for each of the monthly surveys. Inactive data are not considered for emissions calculations, so this step is extremely important. For equipment surveys that request hours of operation, platform surveys were labeled as active if any of the equipment operating hours were greater than zero. Conversely, a platform survey was labeled as inactive if all of the equipment operating hours were zero.

The flare occurrence tables were reviewed to verify the activity status of each survey, although hours of operation are requested in the flare equipment tables. A platform survey was considered active and emissions were calculated if the flare hours of operation were zero, but there was an upset record in the flare occurrence table. This scenario is possible because the operators were asked to report operating hours, excluding process upsets, but to report the number of upsets that occurred during each survey month.

4.5.2 Monthly Total Hours Check

For each month, operating hours were to be provided for most types of equipment. A typical error would be to exceed the maximum hours possible for each month. Alternately, hours of operation may not have been populated. For both of these errors, data were corrected in the same manner by populating with the maximum number of hours possible. The maximum number of hours for months with 31 days (January, March, May, July, August, October, and December) is 744; for months with 30 days (April, June, September, and November), the maximum number of hours is 720. In year 2001, the maximum amount of hours for February (28 days) is 672.

5. DEVELOPMENT OF THE PLATFORM EMISSIONS INVENTORY

5.1 INTRODUCTION

The goal of the current study is to develop a NO_x and SO_2 emission inventory for all oil and gas production-related sources within 100 km of the BNWA. To achieve this goal, ERG revised the draft Breton Oracle DBMS (Coe et al. 2003) to create the updated Breton DBMS. The Breton DBMS imports the activity data described in Sections 3 and 4 of this report, then applies emission factors to calculate emissions from platform sources. The final Breton Oracle DBMS contains platform activity data and other data needed to calculate emissions. Figure 5-1 illustrates the flow of information into and out of the Oracle database.

5.2 EXPANSION OF THE DRAFT BRETON STUDY ORACLE DBMS

The draft Breton DBMS (Coe et al. 2003) was enhanced, creating the final Breton DBMS, by completing the following steps:

- Examining each calculation routine and correcting mathematical and typographical errors;

- Updating emission factors with the latest information in *AP-42* (U.S. EPA 2002);

- Standardizing the calculations to be consistent with the units of measure in *AP-42* (U.S. EPA 2002) ; and

- Comparing calculation methods to current Emission Inventory Improvement Program (EIIP) methods and updating where calculations did not agree with current methods (EIIP 1999).

In addition, MMS provided surrogates for values such as fuel sulfur content, fuel heating value, fuel density, and control efficiency. These surrogate values, shown below, are based on industry averages and/or MMS recommended values. For example, the diesel fuel sulfur content is consistent with MMS' "Spreadsheet for Exploration Plans" (http://www.gomr.mms.gov/homepg/regulate/environ/requirement/html).

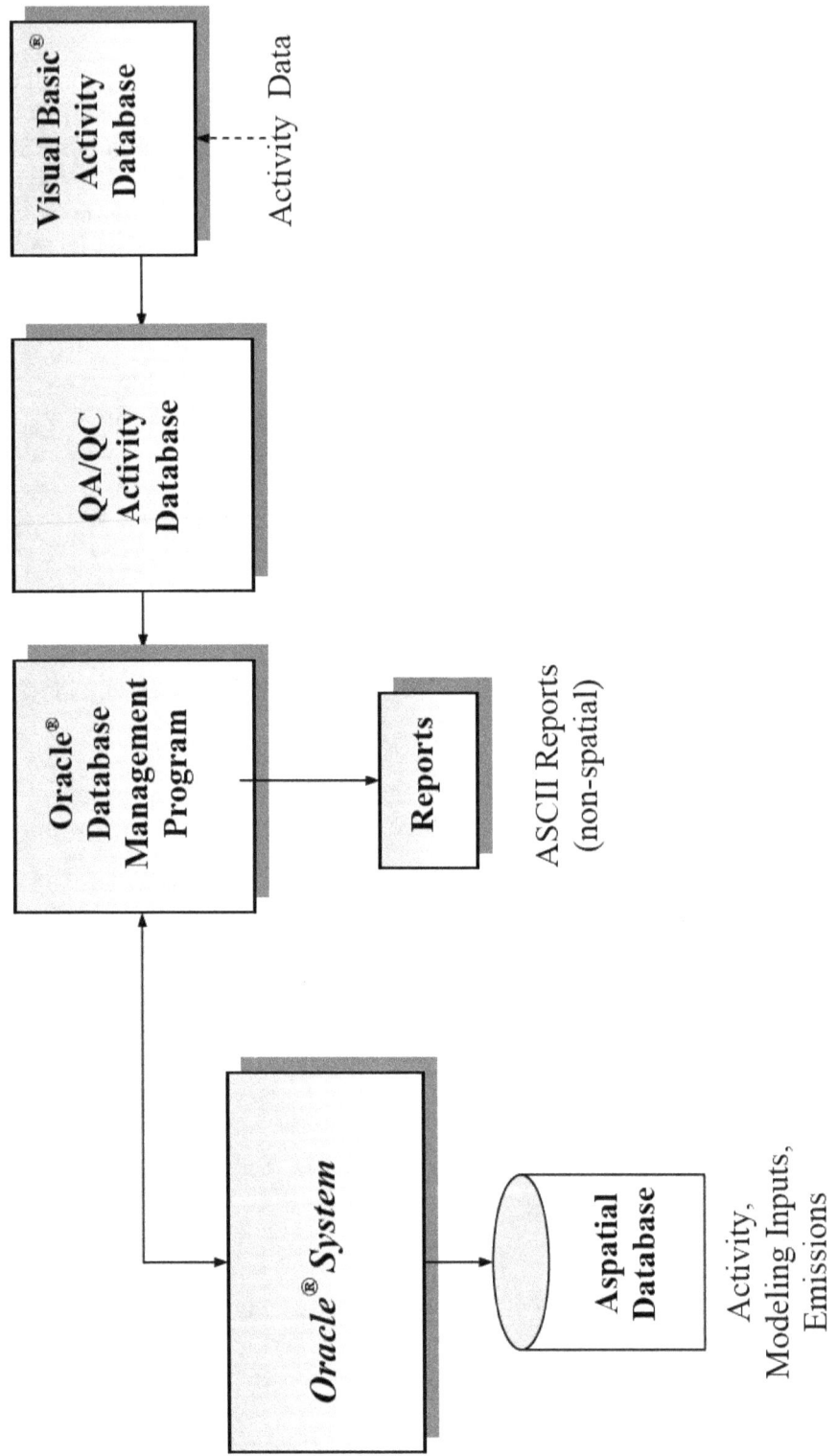

Figure 5-1. Oracle Database Information Flow.

Natural gas hydrogen sulfide (H$_2$S) content	= 3.38 ppmv
Diesel fuel sulfur content	= 0.4 wt%
Natural gas heating value	= 1050 Btu/scf
Diesel fuel heating value	= 19,300 Btu/lb
Diesel fuel density	= 7.1 lb/gal
Gasoline fuel density	= 6.17 lb/gal
Flare efficiency for H$_2$S	= 95%

5.3   EMISSION ESTIMATION PROCEDURES

For the most part, the emission estimating procedures presented in this section build upon the approaches developed for the draft Breton DBMS (Coe et al. 2003). The following sections present a summary of the methods used to calculate NO$_x$ and SO$_2$ emissions from platform sources include in this study.

5.3.1   Amine Units

Some platforms produce natural gas containing unacceptable amounts of hydrogen sulfide. While most platform operators pipe the sour gas onshore for sulfur removal, a few remove the sulfur on the platform using the amine process. Various amine solutions such as diethanolamine (DEA), monoethanolamine (MEA), methyldiethanolamine (MDEA), diglycolamine (DGA) and tertiaryethanolamine (TEA) are used to absorb H$_2$S. After the H$_2$S has been separated out, it is vented, flared, incinerated, or used for feedstock in elemental sulfur production (U.S. DOI, MMS 1995).

Devices that are intended to control H$_2$S emissions, such as sulfur recovery units or flares, will produce emissions of SO$_2$ as a by-product. One third of the H$_2$S is burned to form SO$_2$ and water (EIIP 1999). If a sulfur recovery unit is present, SO$_2$ emissions are calculated as follows.

$$E_{SO_2} = \frac{C_{H2S}}{100} \times Q \times 10^6 \times M_{SO_2} \times \frac{lb \cdot mol}{379.4 \text{ scf}} \times \frac{1 \text{ lb} \cdot mol \text{ SO}_2}{3 \text{ lb} \cdot mol \text{ S}} \times \left(1 - \frac{\%RE}{100}\right)$$

where:

E$_{SO_2}$	=	Controlled SO$_2$ emissions (pounds per month)
C$_{H_2S}$	=	Concentration of H$_2$S in the natural gas, measured at the inlet to the amine unit (percent by volume)
Q	=	Volume of natural gas processed (MMscf/month)
M$_{SO_2}$	=	Molecular weight of SO$_2$ (64 lb/lb·mol)
% RE	=	Recovery efficiency of the sulfur recovery unit

If a flare is present (instead of a sulfur recovery unit), SO_2 emissions are calculated as:

$$E_{SO_2} = \frac{C_{H2S}}{100} \times Q \times 10^6 \times M_{SO_2} \times \frac{lb \cdot mol}{379.4 \, scf} \times \frac{Eff_{SO_2}}{100}$$

where:

E_{SO_2}	=	Controlled SO_2 emissions (pounds per month)
C_{H_2S}	=	Concentration of H_2S in the natural gas, measured at the inlet to the amine unit (percent by volume)
Q	=	Volume of natural gas processed (MMscf)/month
M_{SO_2}	=	Molecular weight of SO_2 (64 lb/lb·mol)
% RE	=	Recovery efficiency of the sulfur recovery unit
Eff_{SO_2}	=	Flare efficiency (%)

5.3.2 Boilers/Heaters/Burners

Boilers, heaters, and burners provide process heat and steam for many processes such as electric generation, glycol dehydrator reboilers, and amine reboiler units (EIIP 1999).

To calculate uncontrolled emissions for liquid-fueled engines (waste oil or diesel) based on fuel use, $E_{fu,liq}$:

$$E_{fu, liq} = EF_{(lb/10^3 \, gal)} \times 10^{-3} \times U_{liq} \div 7.1 \, lb/gal$$

To calculate uncontrolled emissions for gas-fueled engines (natural gas, process gas, or waste gas) based on fuel use, $E_{fu,gas}$:

$$E_{fu,gas} = EF_{(lbs/MMscf)} \times 10^{-3} \times U_{gas}$$

where:

E	=	Emissions (pounds per month)
EF	=	Emission factor (units are shown in parentheses)
U_{liq}	=	Fuel usage (lb/month)
U_{gas}	=	Fuel usage (Mscf/month)

Table 5-1 presents the emission factors used to estimate emissions. These factors come from *AP-42*, Sections 1.3 and 1.4 (U.S. EPA 2002). All boilers are assumed to be wall-fired boilers (no tangential-fired boilers). Emission factors for No. 6 residual oil were used to estimate emissions from waste-oil-fueled units.

Table 5-1. Emission Factors for Boilers/Heaters/Burners.

Pollutant	Emission Factor		
	Uncontrolled	Low NO$_x$ Burner	Flu Gas Recirculation
Diesel Where Max Rated Heat Input ≥ 100 MMBtu/hr (lb/10^3 gal)			
SO$_2$	157 × S	157 × S	157 × S
NO$_x$	24	10	10
Diesel where Max Rated Heat Input < 100 MMBtu/hr (lb/10^3 gal)			
SO$_2$	142 × S	142 × S	142 × S
NO$_x$*	20	20	20
Waste Oil where Max Rated Heat Input ≥ 100 MMBtu/hr (lb/10^3 gal)			
SO$_2$	157 × S	157 × S	157 × S
NO$_x$	47	40	40
Waste Oil where Max Rated Heat Input < 100 MMBtu/hr (lb/10^3 gal)			
SO$_2$	157 × S	157 × S	157 × S
NO$_x$*	55	55	55
Natural Gas or Process Gas, Where Max Rated Heat Input ≥ 100 MMBtu/hr (lb/MMscf)			
SO$_2$	0.6	0.6	0.6
NO$_x$	280	140	100
Natural Gas or Process Gas, Where Max Rated Heat Input < 100 MMBtu/hr (lb/MMscf)			
SO$_2$	0.6	0.6	0.6
NO$_x$	100	50	32

S = Fuel oil sulfur content (weight %)
* NO$_x$ emission reductions for small boilers are typically less significant than for large boilers
 (U.S. EPA 2002)

5.3.3 Diesel and Gasoline Engines

Diesel and gasoline engines are used to run generators, pumps, compressors, and well-drilling equipment. Most of the pollutants emitted from these engines are from the exhaust (U.S. EPA 2002).

If an operator-entered value for total fuel used is available, or if it can be estimated from the default values, then emissions are estimated based upon fuel use. Otherwise, if operating HP and hours operated are both available, then emissions are estimated based upon power output. To calculate uncontrolled emissions based on fuel use:

$$E_{fu} = EF_{(lb/MMBtu)} \times 10^{-6} \times U \times \frac{7.1\,lb}{gal} \times H$$

To calculate uncontrolled emissions based on power output:

$$E_{po} = EF_{(g/hp\text{-}hr)} \times HP \times t \times \frac{lb}{453.6g}$$

where:

E	=	Emissions (pounds per month)
EF	=	Emission factor (units are shown in parentheses)
U	=	Fuel usage (gallons/month)
H	=	Fuel heating value (Btu/lb)
HP	=	Engine horsepower (hp)
t	=	Engine operating time (hr/month)

The following emission factors are used to estimate emissions. These factors come from *AP-42*, Sections 3.3 and 3.4 (U.S. EPA 2002).

Table 5-2. Emission Factors for Gasoline and Diesel Engines.

Pollutant	EF (lb/MMBtu)	EF (g/hp-hr)
Gasoline Engines		
SO_x	0.084	0.268
NO_x	1.63	4.99
Diesel Engines Where Max HP<600		
SO_x	$1.01 \times S$	$3.67 \times S$
NO_x	4.41	14.1
Diesel Engines Where Max HP $\geq$ 600		
SO_x	$1.01 \times S$	$3.67 \times S$
NO_x	3.2	10.9

S = Fuel oil sulfur content (weight %)

5.3.4 Drilling Rigs

Drilling activities associated with an existing facility or from a jack-up rig adjacent to a platform are included because of their emissions associated with combustion engines. Total emissions equal the sum of emissions due to gasoline, diesel, and natural gas fuel usage.

To calculate uncontrolled emissions from gasoline fuel use:

$$E_{gas} = EF_{(lb/MMBtu)} \times 10^{-6} \times U \times Fd \times \frac{20,300 \text{ Btu}}{lb}$$

For diesel fuel use, calculate uncontrolled emissions as follows:

$$E_{die} = EF_{(lb/MMMBtu)} \times 10^{-6} \times U \times Fd \times \frac{19,300 \text{ Btu}}{lb}$$

For natural gas fuel use, calculate uncontrolled emissions as follows:

$$E_{ng} = EF_{(lb/MMscf)} \times 10^{-3} \times U$$

where:

E	=	Emissions (pounds per month)
EF	=	Emission factor (units are shown in parentheses)
Fd	=	Fuel density (lbs/gal)
U	=	Fuel usage (gallons for gasoline and diesel; Mscf for natural gas)

The following emission factors are used to estimate emissions. These factors come from *AP-42*, Sections 3.2, 3.3 and 3.4 (U.S. EPA 2002). Diesel engines are assumed to be ≥ 600 hp. Natural gas engines are assumed to be 4-cycle, and evenly distributed between lean and rich burns (by averaging the emission factors).

Table 5-3. Emission Factors for Engines Used in Drilling Rigs.

Pollutant	Emission Factor
Gasoline (lb/MMBtu)	
SO_x	0.084
NO_x	1.63
Diesel (lb/MMBtu)	
SO_x	$1.01 \times S$
NO_x	3.2
Natural Gas (lb/MMscf)	
SO_2	0.6
NO_x	2467.5

S = Fuel oil sulfur content (weight %)

5.3.5 Flares

A flare is a burning stack used to incinerate pollutants. SO_2 and NO_x emissions occur through combustion of feed stock or the fuel used to maintain the flare. Flares can be used to control emissions from storage tanks, loading operations, glycol dehydration units, vent collection systems, and amine units. Flares usually operate continuously; however some are used only for process upsets (U.S. DOI, MMS 1995).

Flare emissions for NO_x are estimated according to the following equation:

5-7

$$E_{flare} = V_{tot} \times H \times EF_{flare} \div 1000$$

where:

E_{flare}	=	Emissions (pounds per month)
V_{tot}	=	Total volume of gas flared (Mscf) = vol flared + Σ (upset flare feed rate $\times$ hours operated)
H	=	Flare gas heating value (Btu/scf)
EF_{flare}	=	Emission factor for flares (0.068 lb of NO_x/MMBtu)

SO_2 emissions are estimated using to the following equation:

$$E_{flare} = \left(\frac{Eff_F\%}{100\%}\right) \times \frac{10^{-6}}{ppm} \times \frac{m_{SO_2}}{379.4\,scf/lb\cdot mol} \times 1000 \times \left(V' \times C_{H_2S} + \sum_{i=1}^{n} F_i \times t_i \times C_{H_2S,i}\right)$$

where:

E_{flare}	=	Emissions (pounds per month)
$Eff_F\%$	=	Combustion efficiency of the flare (percent)
m_{SO_2}	=	Molecular weight of SO_2 (64 lb/lb·mol)
V'	=	Non-upset volume of gas flared (Mscf)
C_{H_2S}	=	Non-upset concentration of H_2S in the flare gas (ppm)
F_i	=	Upset flare feed rate for occurrence i (Mscf/hr)
t_i	=	Duration of occurrence i (hr)
$C_{H_2S,i}$	=	H_2S concentration for upset occurrence i (ppm)

If the operator indicates there is a continuous flare pilot, pilot light emissions are estimated as follows:

$$E_{pilot} = P \times D \times EF_{pilot} \div 1000$$

where:

E_{Pilot}	=	Pilot emissions (pounds per month)
P	=	Flare feed rate (Mscf/day)
D	=	Number of days per month
EF_{pilot}	=	Emission factor for pilot (100 lbs of NO_x/MMscf)

The emission factors noted above come from *AP-42*, Section 13.5 (U.S. EPA 2002). The following default value is assigned or estimated if the corresponding fields are null:

Pilot Fuel Feed Rate = 2.28 Mscf per day

5.3.6 Natural Gas Engines

Like diesel and gasoline engines, natural gas engines are used to run generators, pumps, compressors, and well-drilling equipment. Most of the pollutants emitted from these engines are from the exhaust (U.S. EPA 2002).

If an operator submitted total fuel usage data or if fuel usage can be estimated from surrogate values, then emissions are calculated based upon fuel usage. Otherwise, equipment HP and hours operated are used to estimate emissions upon power output.

Emissions are calculated based on fuel usage in the following equation:

$$E_{fu} = EF_{(lb/MMBtu)} \times H \times U \times 10^{-3}$$

Emissions are calculated based on power output using the following equation:

$$E_{po} = EF_{(g/hp-hr)} \times HP \times t \times \frac{lb}{453.6g}$$

where:

E	=	Emissions (pounds per month)
EF	=	Emission factor (units are shown in parentheses)
H	=	Gas heat value (Btu/scf)
U	=	Fuel usage (Mscf/month)
HP	=	Engine horsepower (hp)
t	=	Engine operating time (hr/month)

Table 5-4 presents the emission factors used to estimate natural gas engine emissions. These factors come from *AP-42*, Section 3.2 (U.S. EPA 2002).

Table 5-4. Emission Factors for Natural Gas - Powered Engines.

Pollutant	EF_{fu} lb/MMBtu	EF_{po} g/hp-hr
2-cycle Lean Burn		
SO_2*	5.88×10^{-4}	2.00×10^{-3}
NO_x (<90% load)	1.94	6.6
4-cycle Lean Burn		
SO_2*	5.88×10^{-4}	2.00×10^{-3}
NO_x (<90% load)	0.85	2.89
4-cycle Rich Burn		
SO_2	5.88×10^{-4}	2.00×10^{-3}
NO_x (<90% load)	2.27	7.72
Clean Burn		
SO_2	5.88×10^{-4}	2.00×10^{-3}
NO_x	0.59	2.00

* Assumes sulfur content of natural gas is 2,000 gr/10^6 scf (U.S. EPA 2002)

5.3.7 Natural Gas Turbines

A gas turbine is an internal combustion engine that operates with rotary rather than reciprocating motion. Turbines are primarily used to power compressors rather than generate electricity (Boyer and Brodnax 1996). A turbine's operating load has a considerable effect on the resulting emission levels. With reduced loads, there are lower thermal efficiencies and more incomplete combustion (U.S. EPA 2002).

If an operator submitted total fuel usage data or if fuel usage can be estimated from available surrogate data, then emissions were estimated based upon fuel use. Otherwise, HP and hours operated are used to estimate emissions based upon power output.

To calculate emissions based on fuel use:

$$E_{fu} = EF_{(lb/MMBtu)} \times 10^{-3} \times H \times U$$

To calculate emissions based on power output:

$$E_{po} = EF_{(lb/MMBtu)} \times 10^{-6} \times FU \times HP \times t$$

where:

E	=	Emissions (pounds per month)
EF	=	Emission factor (units are shown in parentheses)
H	=	Fuel heating value (Btu/scf)
U	=	Fuel usage (Mscf/month)
HP	=	Turbine horsepower (hp)
t	=	Turbine operating time (hr/month)
FU	=	Average fuel usage (Btu/hp-hr)

The following emission factors are used to estimate emissions. These factors come from *AP-42* Section 3.1 (U.S. EPA 2002).

Table 5-5. Emission Factors for Natural Gas Turbines.

Pollutant	EF (lb/MMBtu)
SO_2	$0.94 \times S$
NO_x	0.32

$S = C_{H2S} \times 1.78 \times 10^{-4}$, % S, where C_{H2S} = ppmv H_2S in fuel.
If not available, EF is 3.4×10^{-3} lb/MMBtu

6. DEVELOPMENT OF THE NON-PLATFORM EMISSIONS INVENTORY

Emission estimates were developed for NO_x and SO_2 for non-platform sources operating within 100 kilometers of the BNWA for the inventory period from September 2000-August 2001. The non-platform sources included in this study are noted below.

OCS oil and gas production sources:

- Drilling vessels;
- Pipelaying operations;
- Platform construction and removal;
- Support helicopters;
- Support vessels; and
- Survey vessels.

Non-OCS oil and gas production sources:

- Commercial fishing;
- Commercial marine vessels; and
- Military vessel operations.

ERG developed the BNWA non-platform emission estimates based on work performed for MMS' *Gulfwide Emission Inventory for the Regional Haze and Ozone Modeling Effort* Study (the Gulfwide Study) (Wilson et al. 2004). These two inventories are significantly different with regard to spatial and temporal issues, as well as the pollutants being considered. As noted above, this study is only concerned with emission sources located in Federal waters 100 km around the BNWA, while the Gulfwide Study includes emission sources located in all of the Federal waters in the Central and Western Gulf of Mexico. Thus, some sources, such as the Louisiana Offshore Oil Platform (LOOP), are not included in this inventory, because the platform and the associated shipping lane approach are located beyond the geographic area of interest. Similarly, the lightering zones included in the Gulfwide Study are not considered in this study, as they too are located outside of the area of interest. Emissions from biogenic/geogenic sources were calculated in the Gulfwide Study for VOCs and nitrous oxide (N_2O). Because VOC and N_2O emissions are not included in the BNWA inventory, biogenic and geogenic sources are not included.

Temporally, the two inventories differ in that the Gulfwide Inventory was developed for base year 2000 (January to December), while the BNWA inventory period covers September 2000 to August 2001. Thus, only four months of Gulfwide data could be matched to the BNWA Inventory's period of interest, and new estimates needed to be developed to represent the period from January to August 2001.

With the exception of support helicopters, the non-platform emission sources in this inventory are vessels or equipment that operate using marine diesel engines. The EPA has developed a new emission factor equation in support of their recent marine diesel rule making (U.S. EPA 2000). The new emission factor equation is based on a regression analysis performed on marine engine test data. For more information on the new marine diesel emission factor equation, see *Analysis of Commercial Marine Vessels Emissions and Fuel Consumption Data* (U.S. EPA 2000). The EPA's emission factor equation uses operating load factors to generate emission factors in terms of kilowatt-hour (kW-hr), as noted below:

$$E\ (g/kW\text{-}hr) = A \times (\text{Load Factors})^{-x} + B$$

where:

E is the power-based emission factor;

Constant A, intercept B, and exponent x were obtained from Table 5-1 of the U.S. EPA (2000) report. All constants needed for this equation are reported in Table 6-1.

Table 6-1. Marine Engine Emission Factor and Fuel Consumption Algorithms (in g/kW-hr, for all marine engines).

Pollutant	Exponent (x)	Intercept (B)	Coefficient (A)
NO_x	1.50	10.45	0.13
SO_2	n/a*	n/a	2.00

* n/a = not applicable
Source: U.S. EPA 2000

For SO_2, it is necessary to first calculate Fuel Consumption using the following equation:

$$\text{Fuel Consumption}\ (g/kW\text{-}hr) = 14.12/(\text{fractional load}) + 205.717$$

It is assumed that diesel fuel, modeled after distillate fuel oil #2, is used in marine applications. Such fuel is assumed to have a sulfur content of 0.4%. This percentage of sulfur in the fuel should be multiplied by the Fuel Consumption calculated above, to estimate the Fuel Sulfur *Flow* as noted below:

$$\text{Fuel Sulfur Flow}\ (g/kW\text{-}hr) = \text{Fuel Consumption}\ (g/kW\text{-}hr) \times 0.004$$

The fuel sulfur flow is thus applied to the following equation to obtain a SO_2 emission rate:

$$SO_2\ \text{Emission Rate}\ (g/kW\text{-}hr) = A \times (\text{Fuel Sulfur Flow in } g/kW\text{-}hr) + B$$

where:

A and B are provided in Table 6-1 above. It should be noted that the A coefficient for the sulfur emission estimate was corrected in this study to 1.998 (which is rounded to 2.00), based on discussions with EPA staff concerning the correct value that should be used.

These emission factors were applied to the hours of operation and typical horsepower (converted to kW) to estimate emissions. Note, this is the same approach used in the Gulfwide Study. For further information about this procedure, refer to Appendices A-J and L in the Gulfwide Inventory report (Wilson et al. 2004). The approaches used to adjust the Gulfwide Inventory data spatially and temporally to match the BNWA Study geographic and time period of interest are summarized below for each non-platform source category.

6.1   OCS OIL AND GAS PRODUCTION RELATED SOURCES

Emission sources included in this group are preliminary drilling operations (exclusive of drilling associated with a platform), the construction or removal of pipelines and oil platforms, the helicopters and vessels that directly provide support to the identification of oil finds, and vessels that ship supplies, equipment, and personnel to and from the platforms.

6.1.1   Drilling Vessels

Drilling vessels are used for exploratory drilling to supplement the geologic information provided by survey vessels. The drilling rig drills a hole in the ocean floor by turning a drill bit attached to lengths of tubular pipe. Several different types of drill rigs operate in the Gulf, including jack-ups, semisubmersibles, submersibles, and drill ships. Drilling rigs vary relative to the water depth where they operate. For example, jack-ups are able to work in water up to 375 feet deep, semisubmersibles and submersibles operate in water with depths of 300 to 2,000 feet, and drill ships operate in waters with depths greater than 2,000 feet.

The Operation and Analysis Branch of the Engineering and Operations Division of MMS provided activity data for drilling rigs by block, which included activity for jack-ups, semisubmersibles, submersibles, and drill ships (Mayes 2002). Only jack-ups and semisubmersibles operated in the Breton area during the period of interest.

Emissions from drilling rigs are associated with the operation of medium- to high-speed marine diesel engines that are used for propulsion, generation of electricity, and operation of mud pumps and draw works. MMS activity data were applied to emission factors derived from EPA marine diesel engine emission equations (U.S. EPA 2000). The EPA's emission factor equation uses operating load factors to generate emission factors in terms of kilowatt-hour (kW-hr), as noted in the equation below:

$$E \ (g/kW\text{-}hr) = A \times (\text{Load Factors})^{-x} + B$$

where:

E is the power-based emission factor;

Constant A, intercept B, and exponent x were obtained from the U.S. EPA (2000) report.

For SO_2 it is necessary to first calculate Fuel Consumption using the following equation:

Fuel Consumption (g/kW-hr) = 14.12/(fractional load) + 205.717

It is assumed that diesel fuel, modeled after distillate fuel oil #2, is used in marine applications. Such fuel is assumed to have a sulfur content of 0.4%. This percentage of sulfur in the fuel should be multiplied by the Fuel Consumption calculated above, to estimate the Fuel Sulfur Flow as noted below:

Fuel Sulfur Flow (g/kW-hr) = Fuel Consumption (g/kW-hr) × 0.004

The fuel sulfur flow is thus applied to the following equation to obtain a SO_2 emission rate:

SO_2 Emission Rate (g/kW-hr) = A × (Fuel Sulfur Flow in g/kW-hr) + B

where:

A and B are dimensionless constants provided in Table 5-1 of the U.S. EPA (2000) report. It should be noted that the A coefficient for the sulfur emission estimate was corrected in this study to 1.998 (which is rounded to 2.00), based on discussions with EPA staff concerning the correct value that should be used.

To use these EPA emission equations, assumptions about vessel horsepower and typical operating loads were obtained from MMS' *Gulf of Mexico Air Quality Study* (GMAQS) (U.S. DOI, MMS 1995). The emission factors developed for drilling rigs are noted in Tables 6-2 and 6-3 for each drill rig type used in Federal waters of the Gulf.

The emission factors shown in Tables 6-2 and 6-3 were applied to the compiled activity data to estimate emissions for the portion of Gulf where MMS has lease blocks. The drilling rig activity data used in this study are based on the specific blocks where drilling activities took place, and the time drilling commenced and concluded. MMS maintains a database of drilling rig activity that includes the location of the drilling activities and the time when drilling was initiated and completed. These data were extracted for the period from September 2000 through August 2001 for lease blocks within the BNWA Study catchment area. These data are summarized in Table 6-4.

Table 6-2. Jack-up Rig Emission Factors.

Typical Vessel HP/kW rating		
	Avg. HP	Avg. kW
Prime	1,660.00	1,237.86
Pumps	1,600.00	1,193.12
Draw works	2,000.00	1,491.40
Total	5,260.00	3,922.38
Operating Load		75%

Emission Factors							
Pollutant	E (g/kW-hr)	Exponent (x)	Intercept (B)	Coefficient (A)	Average kW rating	Kg/hr	lbs/hr
NO_x	10.64	1.50	10.45	0.13	3,922.38	41.75	92.03
SO_2*	1.79	N/A	0.00	2.00	3,922.38	7.02	15.48

*For SO_2 fuel sulfur flow (g/kW-hr) = 14.12/fractional load + 205.717 × fuel sulfur concentration. For this study the fuel sulfur concentration was assumed to be 0.4%

Table 6-3. Semisubmersible Rig Emission Factors.

Typical Vessel HP/kW rating		
	Avg. HP	Avg. kW
Prime	2,034.00	1,516.75
Pumps	1,600.00	1,193.12
Drawworks	3,000.00	2,237.10
Total	6,634.00	4,946.97
Operating Load		75%

Emission Factors							
Pollutant	E (g/kW-hr)	Exponent (x)	Intercept (B)	Coefficient (A)	Average kW rating	Kg/hr	lbs/hr
NO_x	10.64	1.50	10.45	0.13	4,946.97	52.65	116.07
SO_2*	1.79	N/A	0.00	2.00	4,946.97	8.86	19.52

*For SO_2 fuel sulfur flow (g/kW-hr) = 14.12/fractional load + 205.717 × fuel sulfur concentration. For this study the fuel sulfur concentration was assumed to be 0.4%

Table 6-4. Drilling Vessel Activity Data.

Rig Type	Surface Area Code	Surface Block Number	Rig Name	Rig Move on Date	Rig Move off Date	Days	Hours
JU	MP	312	*Chiles Tonala*	10/20/2000	12/6/2000	48	1152
JU	MP	188	*Diamond Ocean Champion*	10/19/2000	11/11/2000	24	576
JU	WD	35	*Diamond Ocean Crusader*	6/16/2001	8/7/2001	53	1272
JU	WD	58	*Diamond Ocean Crusader*	9/1/2000	9/19/2000	19	456
JU	WD	58	*Diamond Ocean Crusader*	10/1/2000	11/27/2000	58	1392
JU	MO	991	*Diamond Ocean Drake*	6/25/2001	8/15/2001	52	1248
JU	VK	158	*Diamond Ocean Drake*	11/1/2000	1/4/2001	65	1560
JU	VK	206	*Diamond Ocean Drake*	1/20/2001	3/23/2001	63	1512
JU	MP	200	*Diamond Ocean Titan*	9/1/2000	10/5/2000	35	840
JU	WD	43	*Diamond Ocean Warwick*	7/28/2001	8/28/2001	32	768
JU	GI	30	*Ensco 54*	1/12/2001	3/1/2001	49	1176
JU	VK	159	*Ensco 54*	3/11/2001	5/2/2001	53	1272
JU	MP	108	*Ensco 60*	7/24/2001	8/17/2001	25	600
JU	MP	150	*Ensco 68*	10/18/2000	12/5/2000	49	1176
JU	MP	20	*Ensco 68*	12/5/2000	3/20/2001	106	2544
JU	MP	131	*Ensco 98*	12/23/2000	1/14/2001	23	552
JU	WD	39	*Falcon Phoenix III*	9/1/2000	9/5/2000	5	120
JU	MP	7	*Falcon Phoenix IV*	9/1/2000	9/24/2000	24	576
JU	MP	239	*Glomar High Island II*	7/15/2001	8/23/2001	40	960
JU	MP	277	*Glomar Main Pass IV*	9/5/2000	10/25/2000	51	1224
JU	MP	114	*Marine 200*	10/13/2000	11/19/2000	38	912
JU	MP	114	*Marine 200*	10/13/2000	11/30/2000	49	1176
JU	MP	20	*Marine 300*	10/27/2000	10/30/2000	4	96
JU	MP	226	*Marine 300*	9/10/2000	10/27/2000	48	1152
JU	WD	59	*Marine 300*	11/1/2000	12/11/2000	41	984
JU	MP	275	*Marine 303*	6/3/2001	7/19/2001	47	1128
JU	MP	164	*Marine IV*	1/13/2001	1/24/2001	12	288
JU	WD	117	*Marine XV*	11/1/2000	11/10/2000	10	240
JU	SP	38	*Marine XVIII*	11/28/2000	2/21/2001	86	2064
JU	SP	38	*Marine XVIII*	2/21/2001	2/22/2001	2	48
JU	SP	38	*Marine XVIII*	2/22/2001	5/19/2001	87	2088
JU	SP	38	*Marine XVIII*	5/19/2001	7/31/2001	74	1776
JU	WD	59	*Marine XVIII*	9/19/2000	11/28/2000	71	1704
JU	VK	565	*Noble Johnnie Hoffman*	11/11/2000	1/12/2001	63	1512
JU	BS	54	*Parker 14-J15*	4/5/2001	5/3/2001	29	696
JU	MP	108	*Parker 14-J15*	7/24/2001	7/24/2001	1	24
JU	BS	41	*Parker 15-J*	6/2/2001	7/6/2001	35	840
JU	WD	23	*Pool Ranger V*	9/1/2000	10/29/2000	59	1416
JU	MP	181	*Pride Alabama*	7/26/2001	8/15/2001	21	504
JU	MP	62	*Pride California*	4/6/2001	4/28/2001	23	552
JU	VK	169	*Pride Kansas*	3/22/2001	4/15/2001	25	600
JU	VK	340	*Pride Kansas*	4/15/2001	5/19/2001	35	840
JU	MO	864	*Pride Wyoming*	2/11/2001	3/10/2001	28	672

Table 6-4. Drilling Vessel Activity Data (Continued).

Rig Type	Surface Area Code	Surface Block Number	Rig Name	Rig Move on Date	Rig Move off Date	Days	Hours
JU	MO	908	*Pride Wyoming*	1/21/2001	2/10/2001	21	504
JU	MP	159	*Pride Wyoming*	12/11/2000	1/12/2001	33	792
JU	MP	163	*Pride Wyoming*	1/13/2001	1/20/2001	8	192
JU	MP	61	*Pride Wyoming*	10/15/2000	11/20/2000	37	888
JU	MP	61	*Pride Wyoming*	11/1/2000	11/14/2000	14	336
JU	MP	61	*Pride Wyoming*	11/20/2000	12/10/2000	21	504
JU	SP	90	*Pride Wyoming*	11/14/2000	11/15/2000	2	48
JU	MP	7	*R&B Falcon 200*	4/8/2001	5/3/2001	26	624
JU	GI	31	*R&B Falcon 203*	9/4/2000	11/20/2000	78	1872
JU	MP	86	*R&B Falcon 251*	10/23/2000	12/1/2000	40	960
JU	MP	86	*R&B Falcon 251*	12/1/2000	12/21/2000	21	504
JU	GI	33	*R&B Falcon 252*	2/3/2001	4/3/2001	60	1440
JU	MP	164	*Rowan Houston*	8/10/2001	8/12/2001	3	72
JU	MP	217	*Rowan-Alaska*	10/5/2000	10/22/2000	18	432
JU	MP	233	*Rowan-Alaska*	10/23/2000	2/5/2001	106	2544
JU	MP	86	*Sundowner Dolphin 106*	6/13/2001	6/30/2001	18	432
JU	MP	86	*Sundowner Dolphin 106*	6/30/2001	7/7/2001	8	192
SS	VK	739	*Borgny Dolphin*	9/1/2000	9/8/2000	8	192
SS	MP	145	*Cal Dive Uncle John*	1/21/2001	3/21/2001	60	1440
SS	VK	739	*Diamond Ocean Ambassador*	7/23/2001	8/31/2001	40	960
SS	MC	321	*Diamond Ocean Concord*	9/1/2000	9/20/2000	20	480
SS	VK	737	*Diamond Ocean Concord*	6/25/2001	8/10/2001	47	1128
SS	WD	148	*Diamond Ocean Endeavor*	5/21/2001	8/31/2001	103	2472
SS	SP	90	*Diamond Ocean Lexington*	11/17/2000	12/3/2000	17	408
SS	MC	278	*Diamond Ocean Saratoga*	2/13/2001	5/22/2001	99	2376
SS	MC	322	*Diamond Ocean Saratoga*	5/22/2001	7/8/2001	48	1152
SS	MC	322	*Diamond Ocean Saratoga*	7/8/2001	8/13/2001	37	888
SS	SP	52	*Diamond Ocean Saratoga*	1/16/2001	2/12/2001	28	672
SS	MC	243	*Ensco 7500*	9/1/2000	8/31/2001	365	8760
SS	MC	199	*Glomar Celtic Sea*	10/10/2000	11/10/2000	32	768
SS	MC	199	*Glomar Celtic Sea*	11/11/2000	1/4/2001	55	1320
SS	MC	243	*Glomar Celtic Sea*	2/17/2001	3/6/2001	18	432
SS	VK	863	*Transocean 96*	5/5/2001	5/28/2001	24	576

The drilling operation emissions were spatially allocated to the lease blocks where drilling occurred. Figure 6-1 maps the location of all of the drilling rigs.

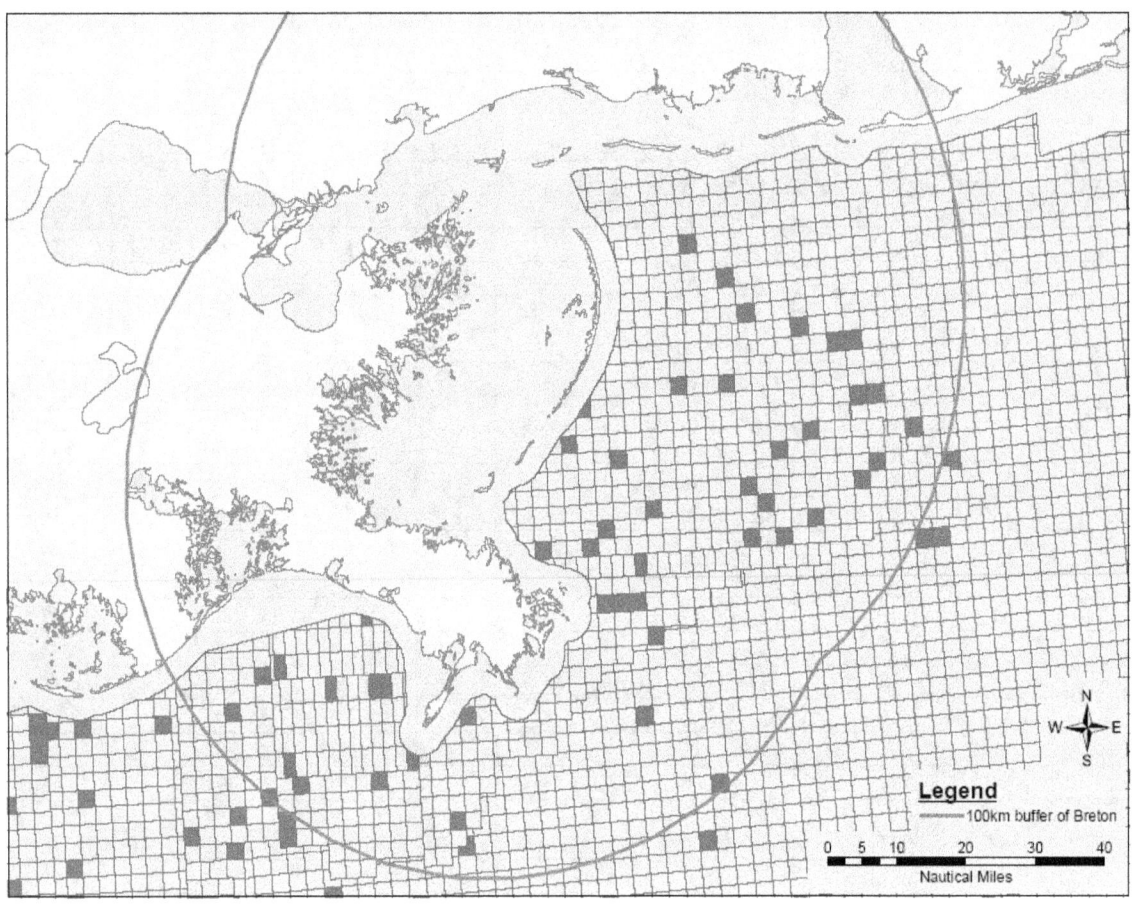

Figure 6-1. Location of Drilling Operations and MMS Lease Blocks for 2000.

6.1.2 Pipelaying Operations

Product from oil platforms is generally transported to shore via pipeline. New pipelines are constantly being laid linking new platforms to shore. Pipelines also require occasional maintenance and repair. To install, maintain, or replace sections of pipeline necessitates considerable vessel support. In the GMAQS, the number of vessels needed to lay a given length of pipe in 24 hours was estimated (U.S. DOI, MMS 1995). From these assumptions, it was calculated that it takes 0.4 total vessel hours to lay one foot of pipe. This "vessel hours per foot" value was applied to the geographic information system (GIS) data provided by the MMS Pipeline Section to estimate hours of operation. The MMS data documents the length and location of individual sections constructed or maintained from September 2000 to August 2001 (Froomer 2002, Froomer 2003). These data were mapped to individual lease blocks in the BNWA Study catchment area using GIS tools. The total length of pipeline constructed or maintained within a lease block were calculated for each lease block, along with the total vessel hours included in these activities, based on the following equation:

$$T_{pi} = \Sigma \ (L_i \times 0.4 \ hrs/ft)$$

where:

$$T_{pi} \quad = \quad \text{Total vessel time involved in pipelaying or maintenance for lease block i (hrs)}$$

$$L_i \quad = \quad \text{Length of individual pipe segment within the boundaries of lease block i (ft)}$$

Emissions associated with pipelaying vessels are attributed to the operation of the primary diesel engine used for propulsion and other smaller diesel engines that are used to run generators, air compressors, welding equipment, or small cranes and winches. Releases of gas or oil from pipelines that required repair or accidental releases during construction or maintenance were not considered in this study. Combustion emissions were estimated by using the EPA's emission factor equation (U.S. EPA 2000). This emission factor equation uses operating load factors to generate emission factors in terms of kilowatt-hour (kW-hr), as noted in the equation below:

$$E \text{ (g/kW-hr)} = A \times (\text{Load Factors})^{-x} + B$$

where:

E is the power-based emission factor;

Constant A, intercept B, and exponent x were obtained from the U.S. EPA (2000) report. For SO_2 it is necessary to first calculate Fuel Consumption using the following equation:

$$\text{Fuel Consumption (g/kW-hr)} = 14.12/(\text{fractional load}) + 205.717$$

It is assumed that diesel fuel, modeled after distillate fuel oil #2, is used in marine applications. Such fuel is assumed to have a sulfur content of 0.4%. This percentage of sulfur in the fuel should be multiplied by the Fuel Consumption calculated above, to estimate the Fuel Sulfur Flow as noted below:

$$\text{Fuel Sulfur Flow (g/kW-hr)} = \text{Fuel Consumption (g/kW-hr)} \times 0.004$$

The fuel sulfur flow is thus applied to the following equation to obtain a SO_2 emission rate:

$$SO_2 \text{ Emission Rate (g/kW-hr)} = A \times (\text{Fuel Sulfur Flow in g/kW-hr}) + B$$

where:

A and B are dimensionless constants provided in Table 5-1 of the U.S. EPA (2000) report. It should be noted that the A coefficient for the sulfur emission estimate was corrected in this study to 1.998 (which is rounded to 2.00), based on discussions with EPA staff concerning the correct value that should be used.

Assumptions about average horsepower and load factors were obtained from the GMAQS (U.S. DOI, MMS 1995) and applied to EPA emission equations (U.S. EPA 2000) to obtain an hourly emission factors. The pipelaying emission factors used in this inventory are noted in Table 6-5.

Table 6-5. Emission Factors for Pipelaying Vessels.

Operating Load	Avg. HP	Avg. kW	Total Hrs per Foot					
75%	1200.00	894.84	0.40					

Emission Factors for Pipelaying Vessels (per foot of pipe)								
Pollutant	E (g/kW-hr)	Exponent (x)	Intercept (B)	Coefficient (A)	Avg kW rating	lbs/hr	Hrs/ft	Emission Factor (lbs/ft)
NOₓ	10.64	1.50	10.45	0.13	894.84	21.00	0.40	8.40
SO₂*	1.79	N/A	0.00	2.00	894.84	3.53	0.40	1.41

*For SO_2 fuel sulfur flow (g/kW-hr) = 14.12/fractional load + 205.717 × fuel sulfur concentration. For this study the fuel sulfur concentration was assumed to be 0.4%

To estimate NO_x and SO_2 emissions, these hourly emission factors were applied to the calculated hours of operation noted in Table 6-6.

Table 6-6. Pipelaying Activity Data.

Projection ID	Block ID	Sum of Segment Lengths (feet)	Hours
LA10	7	11,833.92	47,335.70
LA10	18	736.55	2,946.19
LA10	103	817.19	3,268.77
LA10A	164	12,485.86	49,943.44
LA10A	178	16,278.48	65,113.91
LA10A	259	42,159.02	168,636.09
LA10A	275	8,731.46	34,925.85
LA10A	276	14,171.16	56,684.65
LA10A	277	14,172.90	56,691.60
LA10A	278	14,170.37	56,681.50
LA10A	279	5,638.88	22,555.51
LA7	23	23,313.42	93,253.67
LA7	32	11,298.92	45,195.67
LA7	33	17,970.44	71,881.76

Table 6-6. Pipelaying Activity Data (Continued).

Projection ID	Block ID	Sum of Segment Lengths (feet)	Hours
LA7	43	3,176.97	12,707.87
LA7	47	2,972.83	11,891.34
LA7	48	3,995.83	15,983.33
LA8	23	1,403.44	5,613.78
LA8	59	5,060.17	20,240.68
LA8	109	3,235.17	12,940.68
LA9	28	4,451.80	17,807.22
LA9A	89	14,976.41	59,905.64
LA9A	90	1,238.85	4,955.38
LA9A	92	17,931.50	71,725.98
LA9A	93	14,776.28	59,105.12
LA9A	96	14,766.83	59,067.32
NH16-04	820	11,823.56	47,294.23
NH16-04	864	8,704.43	34,817.72
NH16-04	865	11,609.02	46,436.09
NH16-04	908	6,742.72	26,970.87
NH16-04	909	11,244.36	44,977.43
NH16-04	910	15,462.04	61,848.16
NH16-04	911	11,405.68	45,622.70
NH16-04	955	5,734.88	22,939.50
NH16-04	956	17,288.81	69,155.25
NH16-04	957	8,445.54	33,782.15
NH16-04	1001	10,254.82	41,019.29
NH16-04	1002	17,788.12	71,152.49
NH16-07	34	447.47	1,789.90
NH16-07	35	17,707.48	70,829.92
NH16-07	36	16,086.91	64,347.64
NH16-07	37	3,677.49	14,709.97
NH16-07	81	12,392.29	49,569.16
NH16-07	82	16,103.08	64,412.34
NH16-07	251	22,897.01	91,588.06
NH16-07	252	12,857.45	51,429.79
NH16-07	296	32,540.29	130,161.15
NH16-07	340	28,320.31	113,281.23

Table 6-6. Pipelaying Activity Data (Continued).

Projection ID	Block ID	Sum of Segment Lengths (feet)	Hours
NH16-07	694	58,148.62	232,594.49
NH16-07	738	63,885.01	255,540.03
NH16-07	739	2,652.13	10,608.53
NH16-08	45	16,085.63	64,342.52
NH16-08	46	4.30	17.19
NH16-10	321	11,746.56	46,986.22
NH16-10	364	9,109.45	36,437.80
NH16-10	365	9,768.96	39,075.85
NH16-10	408	15,837.40	63,349.61
NH16-10	452	1.80	7.22
	Total	768,538.29	3,074,153.15

Pipelaying emissions were mapped to the links provided by the MMS and are provided in Figure 6-2.

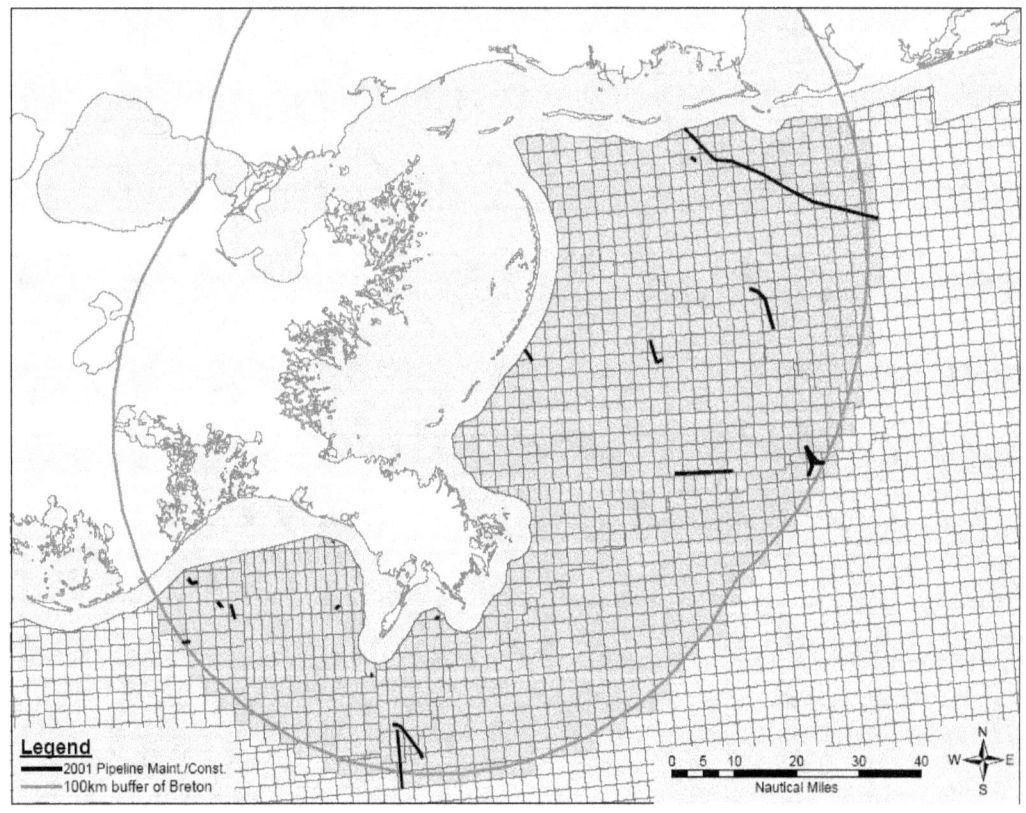

Figure 6-2. Pipeline Locations and MMS Lease Blocks.

6.1.3   Platform Construction and Removal

A variety of vessels are needed to transfer equipment, materials, and structural platform components, as well as workers and technicians, during the construction and removal of offshore oil platforms. The methods used to estimate emissions from these vessels were adapted from another MMS study, *Emission Inventories of OCS Production and Development Activities in the Gulf of Mexico – Final Report* (Coe et al. 2003). As the vessels involved in platform construction and removal activities are similar to support vessels (see Section 6.1.5) many of the same assumptions about vessel characteristics and operations were used to estimate emissions.

Platforms that were installed or removed during the period from September 2000 to August 2001 were identified using MMS' platform structure database. Additional data were provided by MMS quantifying the water depth at the platform and the number of pilings associated with individual platforms. This information was used in conjunction with data included in Coe et al. (2003), to estimate the total vessel hours associated with platform construction and removal. Assumptions about typical vessel horsepower and operating loads used in the support vessel calculations were also used to develop emission factors for vessels associated with this source category using the EPA marine diesel emission factor equation (U.S. EPA 2000). The EPA's emission factor equation uses operating load factors to generate emission factors in terms of kilowatt-hour (kW-hr), as noted in the equation below:

$$E \text{ (g/kW-hr)} = A \times (\text{Load Factors})^{-x} + B$$

where:

E is the power-based emission factor;

Constant A, intercept B, and exponent x were obtained from the U.S. EPA (2000) report.

For SO_2, it is necessary to first calculate Fuel Consumption using the following equation:

$$\text{Fuel Consumption (g/kW-hr)} = 14.12/(\text{fractional load}) + 205.717$$

It is assumed that diesel fuel, modeled after distillate fuel oil #2, is used in marine applications. Such fuel is assumed to have a sulfur content of 0.4%. This percentage of sulfur in the fuel should be multiplied by the Fuel Consumption calculated above, to estimate the Fuel Sulfur Flow as noted below:

$$\text{Fuel Sulfur Flow (g/kW-hr)} = \text{Fuel Consumption (g/kW-hr)} \times 0.004$$

The fuel sulfur flow is thus applied to the following equation to obtain a SO_2 emission rate:

$$SO_2 \text{ Emission Rate (g/kW-hr)} = A \times (\text{Fuel Sulfur Flow in g/kW-hr}) + B$$

where:

A and B are dimensionless constants provided in Table 5-1 of the U.S. EPA (2000) report. It should be noted that the A coefficient for the sulfur emission estimate was corrected in this study to 1.998 (which is rounded to 2.00), based on discussions with EPA staff concerning the correct value that should be used.

The construction and removal emission factors used for each type of vessel involved in these operations are noted in Table 6-7.

Table 6-7. Platform Construction and Removal Emission Factors.

Pollutant	E (g/kW-hr)	Exponent (x)	Intercept (B)	Coefficient (A)	kW	kg/hr	lbs/hr
Barges							
NOx	10.76	1.50	10.45	0.13	229.70	2.47	5.45
SO2*	1.84	N/A	0.00	2.00	229.70	0.42	0.93
Crew Boats							
NOx	10.61	1.50	10.45	0.13	357.90	3.80	8.37
SO2*	1.77	N/A	0.00	2.00	357.90	0.63	1.40
Supply Boats							
NOx	10.76	1.50	10.45	0.13	647.30	6.96	15.35
SO2*	1.84	N/A	0.00	2.00	647.30	1.19	2.63
Tug Boats							
NOx	10.76	1.50	10.45	0.13	1665.90	17.93	39.52
SO2*	1.85	N/A	0.00	2.00	1665.90	3.08	6.78

Load factors used: barge=0.55; crew=0.865; supply=0.55; tug=0.5445
*For SO2 fuel sulfur flow (g/kW-hr) = 14.12/fractional load + 205.717 × fuel sulfur concentration
For this study the fuel sulfur concentration was assumed to be 0.4%

To calculate total platform construction or removal emissions, these hourly emission factors were applied to the estimate of total vessel hours of operation for individual platforms that were constructed or removed during the study period, as noted in Table 6-8.

Table 6-8. Platform Construction/Removal Activity Data.

Area Code	Block Number	Complex ID	Install Date	Removal Date	Water Depth	Duration (days)	Duration (hours)
BS	54	949	05/02/01		20	9	216
GI	31	795	09/26/00		75	6	144
GI	33	870	01/17/01		82	9	216
GI	41	766	11/15/00		100	6	144
GI	79	23845	01/01/90	1/15/01	203	9	216
MO	992	711	12/5/00		91	9	216
MP	124	23441	01/01/88	11/03/00	78	9	216
MP	129	23453	01/01/88	10/13/00	95	9	216
MP	164	948	07/18/01		135	9	216
MP	20	851	12/08/00		34	9	216
MP	275	900	05/19/01		231	9	216
MP	61	928	05/13/01		91	10	240
MP	7	809	09/24/00		39	10	240
MP	86	842	11/29/00		70	9	216
MP	86	861	12/21/00		75	6	144
MP	95	23429	01/01/88	06/26/01	55	9	216
VK	122	31020	09/29/96	04/19/01	110	6	144
VK	123	31017	10/04/96	05/06/01	115	6	144
VK	155	24223	04/20/95	09/29/00	97	9	216
VK	33	31015	09/09/96	04/26/01	105	6	144
VK	35	70006	01/25/97	04/21/01	115	9	216
VK	70	256	07/30/98	07/31/01	105	6	144
WD	28	20192	02/28/01		37	6	144
WD	59	856	03/06/01		60	6	144
WD	78	174	05/02/99	04/24/01	87	6	144
					Total	197	4,728

Emissions for each platform were attributed to the lease block where the platform was located as noted in Figure 6-3. Only those platform construction and removal activities that occurred within the BNWA Study catchment area were included in this inventory of non-platform sources.

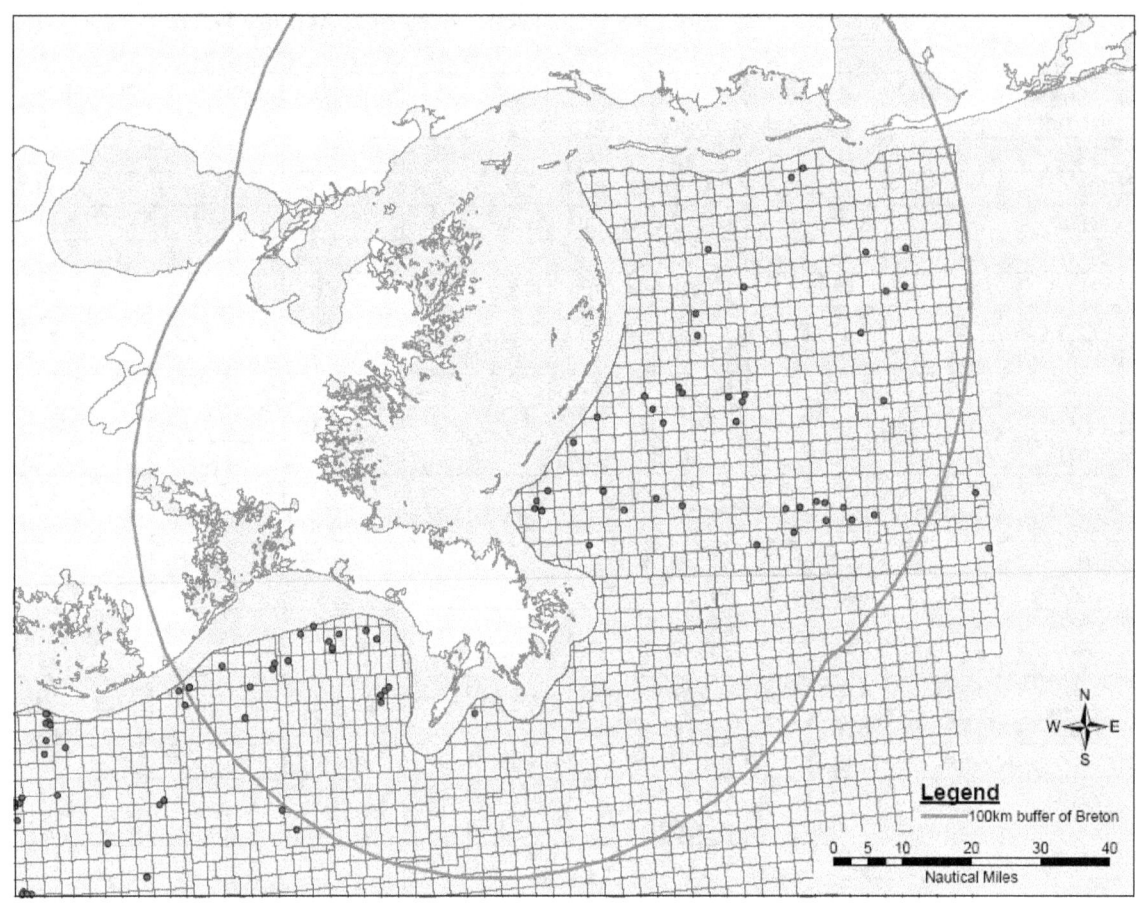

Figure 6-3. Location of Platform Construction and Removal.

6.1.4   Support Helicopters

Helicopters are used extensively in the Gulf to move light supplies and personnel to and from platforms. Total activity data for 2000 and 2001 for the Gulf area were obtained from the *Helicopter Safety Advisory Conference's (HSAC) Gulf of Mexico Offshore Helicopter Operations and Safety Review* (HSAC 2001). This reference provided data on the number of helicopter trips taken, number of passengers carried, and duration of trips. The activity data were disaggregated into single engine, twin engine, and heavy twin engine helicopters. It was assumed that the proportion of single, twin, and heavy twin helicopters operating in the entire Gulf is similar to the proportion of single, twin, and heavy twin helicopters operating in the BNWA study area. It should also be noted that lease-block specific helicopter data are not readily available. Helicopter landing and takeoff (LTO) activity within the BNWA was estimated by extracting annual helicopter activity data from the Gulfwide study, as summarized in Table 6-9. Actual activity for the BNWA may be different than the estimated activity noted.

Table 6-9. Summary of Helicopter Activity Data.

Helicopter Type	Single	Twin	Heavy Twin	Total
Estimated LTOs	32,864	15,535	1,280	49,679

The average trip length was relatively short (16 minutes) (HSAC 2001); it is assumed that helicopters typically hop from platform to platform, therefore the emission estimates are based on a short LTO cycle that is appropriate for the documented average trip length. Activity was estimated by applying the number of helicopter trips to the average trip time to yield total hours of operation.

The helicopter emission factors were obtained from multiple sources including the *Final Air Quality Management Plan, 1991 Revision, Final Technical Report III-G, 1987 Aircraft Emission Inventory in the South Coast Air Basin* developed by the California South Coast Air Quality Management District (SCAQMD 1991). Staff at the California Air Resources Board noted that these emission factors have not been updated since 1991. Additional helicopter emission factors were obtained from EPA's *Procedures for Emission Inventory Preparation Volume IV: Mobile Sources* (U.S. EPA 1992), as well as data from the Allison helicopter engine manufacturer (Allison 2002), and helicopter test data from the Department of the Navy's *Environmental Assessments* (Dept. of the Navy 1999*)*. Staff at the EPA's Office of Transportation and Air Quality (OTAQ) were contacted to insure that all data sources of helicopter emission factors were identified in this effort.

As discussed in the Gulfwide Inventory Report (Wilson et al. 2004), the emission factors were disaggregated into the helicopter types used in the HSAC's activity data LTO-based emission factors for each helicopter type were averaged providing the emission factors used in this study. These average emission factors are summarized in Table 6-10. The data obtained for military helicopters were not included in the average because some of the emission factors were more than an order of magnitude different from the factors obtained from other data sources and a credible explanation for the difference could not be provided; also most of the helicopters used to support oil platform activities are commercial, not military helicopters.

Table 6-10. Average Helicopter Emission Factors.

Helicopter Type	NO_x (lb/LTO)	SO_2 (lb/LTO)
Single-Engine	0.55	0.19
Twin-Engine	4.01	0.33
Heavy Twin-Engine	17.40	1.10

The helicopter activity data noted in Table 6-9 were applied to the emission factors developed in this study to estimate emissions from this source category. Helicopter emissions were apportioned by assigning emissions to lease blocks with active platforms that have heliports (see Figure 6-4), as most of the emissions associated with support helicopters occurs while the craft is near or at the platform. Spatial allocation of helicopter emissions was made using the equation below.

$$E_{Hi} = E_H \times (P_{Hi}/P_{HT})$$

where:

E_{Hi}	=	Support helicopter emissions associated with lease block i
E_H	=	Total helicopter emissions
P_{Hi}	=	Number of platforms with heliports in lease block i
P_{HT}	=	Total number of platforms with heliports

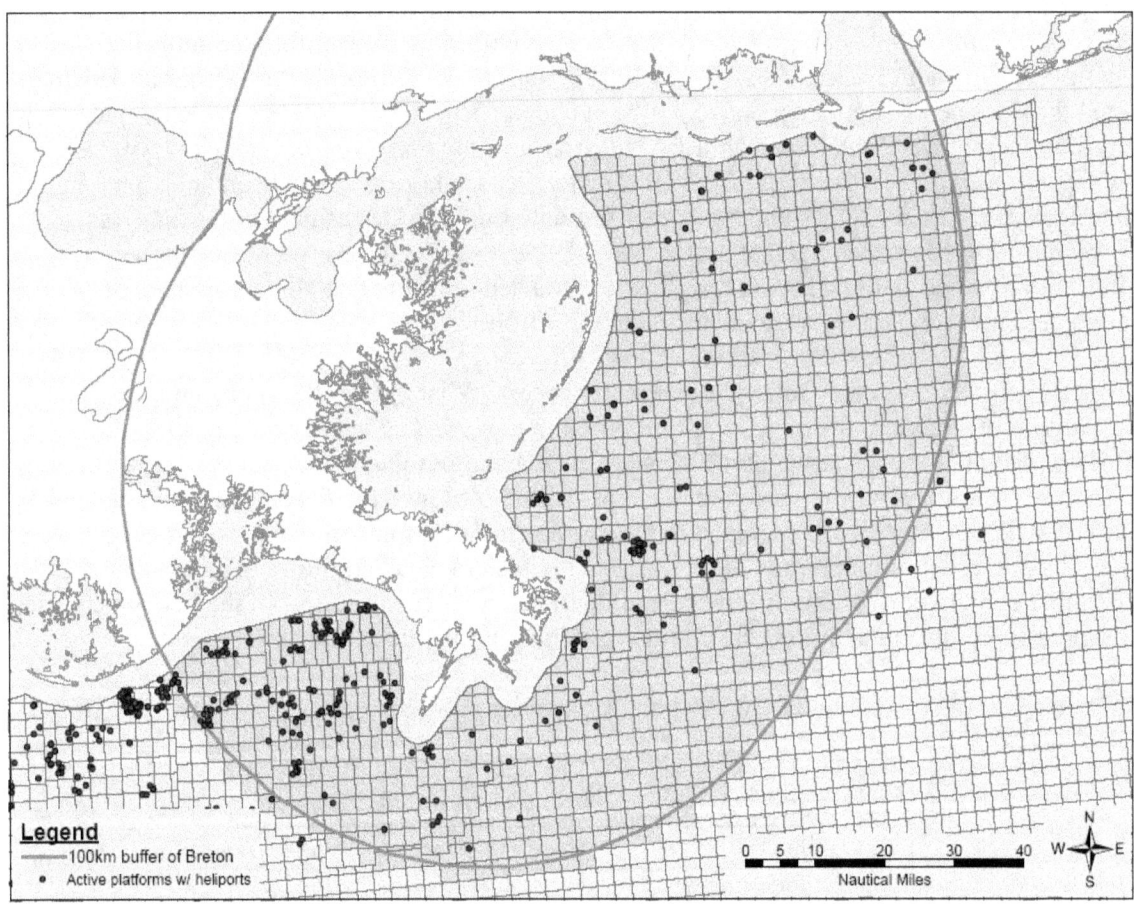

Figure 6-4. Location of Active Platforms with Helipads.

6.1.5 Support Vessels

Support vessels include crew boats that transport workers to and from work sites, supply vessels that carry supplies to offshore sites, and tugs and barges that transport heavy equipment and supplies. Emissions associated with support vessels are attributed to the operation of the primary diesel engine used for propulsion and other smaller diesel engines that are used to run generators or small cranes and winches for loading and unloading the vessels.

Data characterizing the support vessel fleet for 2000 or 2001 are not available. The number of support vessels for the year 1992 was obtained from the GMAQS (U.S. DOI, MMS 1995). In the GMAQS it was estimated that approximately 3,400 platforms were in operation (in 1992). It should be noted that the 1992 support vessel survey had a response rate of 64%, such that actual vessel numbers maybe larger than those reported in the study. Currently, MMS estimates that the number of active platforms in 2000 was 4,003, an increase of approximately 17% from 1992 (U.S. DOI, MMS, 2004). Note that this increased number of platforms is not related to the number of platforms that reported in the Gulfwide Study (Wilson et al. 2004). It is based on the MMS estimates of active platforms. It is assumed that as the number of platforms increase, the support vessel fleet increases proportionally. Therefore, the 1992 support vessel fleet was increased 17% in order to approximate the size of the support vessel fleet in 2000/2001. The GMAQS assumed that support vessels operate 21 hours per day; this assumption was also used in this study. The vessel population estimate and the average hours of operation were used to calculate the total annual hours that support vessels operate.

The amount of time that each type of support vessel typically spends in each of the operating modes (i.e., hoteling, maneuvering, and cruising), the load factor associated with each operating mode, and typical engine horsepower rating was assumed to be the same in 2000 and 2001 as was documented in the GMAQS (U.S. DOI, MMS 1995). The operating mode times, load factors, and typical horsepower ratings were applied to the EPA marine diesel engine equations to obtain representative emission factors. The EPA's emission factor equation provides emission factors in terms of kilowatt-hour (kW-hr), as noted in the equation below:

$$E \text{ (g/kW-hr)} = A \times (\text{Load Factors})^{-x} + B$$

where:

E is the power-based emission factor;

Constant A, intercept B, and exponent x were obtained from the U.S. EPA (2000) report.

For SO_2, it is necessary to first calculate Fuel Consumption using the following equation:

$$\text{Fuel Consumption (g/kW-hr)} = 14.12/(\text{fractional load}) + 205.717$$

It is assumed that diesel fuel, modeled after distillate fuel oil #2, is used in marine applications. Such fuel is assumed to have a sulfur content of 0.4%. This percentage of sulfur in the fuel should be multiplied by the Fuel Consumption calculated above, to estimate the Fuel Sulfur Flow as noted below:

$$\text{Fuel Sulfur Flow (g/kW-hr)} = \text{Fuel Consumption (g/kW-hr)} \times 0.004$$

The fuel sulfur flow is thus applied to the following equation to obtain a SO_2 emission rate:

$$SO_2 \text{ Emission Rate (g/kW-hr)} = A \times (\text{Fuel Sulfur Flow in g/kW-hr}) + B$$

where:

A and B are dimensionless constants provided in Table 5-1 of the U.S. EPA (2000) report. It should be noted that the A coefficient for the sulfur emission estimate was corrected in this study to 1.998 (which is rounded to 2.00), based on discussions with EPA staff concerning the correct value that should be used.

The support vessel emission factors used in the BNWA Inventory are noted in Table 6-11.

Table 6-11. Support Vessel Emission Factors.

Pollutant	E (g/kW-hr)	Exponent (x)	Intercept (B)	Coefficient (A)	kW	kg/hr	lbs/hr
Barges							
NO_x	10.76	1.50	10.45	0.13	229.70	2.47	5.45
SO_2*	1.84	N/A	0.00	2.00	229.70	0.42	0.93
Crew Boats							
NO_x	10.61	1.50	10.45	0.13	357.90	3.80	8.37
SO_2*	1.77	N/A	0.00	2.00	357.90	0.63	1.40
Supply Boats							
NO_x	10.76	1.50	10.4496	0.13	647.30	6.96	15.35
SO_2*	1.84	N/A	0.00	2.00	647.30	1.19	2.63
Tug Boats							
NO_x	10.76	1.50	10.45	0.13	1665.90	17.93	39.52
SO_2*	1.85	N/A	0.00	2.00	1665.90	3.08	6.78

Load factors used: barge=0.55; crew=0.865; supply=0.55; tug=0.5445
*For SO_2 fuel sulfur flow (g/kW-hr) = 14.12/fractional load + 205.717 × fuel sulfur concentration
For this study the fuel sulfur concentration was assumed to be 0.4%

These emission factors were applied to the activity data as noted in Table 6-12 to estimate emissions. It was assumed that the vessel types associated with the Gulf support vessel fleet are similar to the vessel types that operate in the vicinity of the BNWA. Operating hours were derived from support vessels operating hours estimated in the Gulfwide Inventory (Wilson et al. 2004). Using GIS tools, activity data for only the lease blocks associated with the BNWA were extracted from the Gulfwide Inventory data set. In the Gulfwide Inventory, support vessel activity were disaggregated into platform hoteling and underway activities.

Table 6-12. Support Vessel Activity by Vessel Type.

Vessel Types	Estimated Number of Vessels	Assumed Hours of Operation (hrs/day)	Total Annual Hours of Operation
Barges	3	21	22,995
Crew Boats	10	21	76,650
Supply Boats	36	21	275,940
Tugs	6	21	45,990
Total	55		421,575

As noted earlier, it was assumed that 25 percent of emissions are associated with hoteling operations at the platform. Platform hoteling emissions were assigned equally to all active platforms. Underway support vessel emissions were spatially apportioned based on the location of active offshore platform and the location of the closest port using the equation below:

$$E_{SVi} = E_{SV} \times (S_{li}/S_{lt})$$

where:

E_{SVi} = Support vessel emissions associated with lease block i

E_{SV} = Total underway emissions associated with support vessels

S_{li} = Sum of the lengths of all support vessel fairways within the boundaries of the lease block i

S_{lt} = Total sum of all support vessel fairways in the Central and Western areas of the GOM

Only those support vessel activities that occurred within the BNWA inventory catchment area were included in this inventory of non-platform sources (see Figure 6-5). Actual emissions for lease blocks closer to shore are probably overestimated using the above methods, as it is assumed that support vessels only travel between local ports and specific platforms. Support vessels may actually travel to multiple platforms before returning to port. At this time, data are not readily available to map actual support vessel routes.

6.1.6 Survey Vessels

Survey vessels are used in the Gulf to map geologic formations and seismic properties. These survey mapping activities are needed to evaluate potential oil reserves in the Gulf. The most common survey technique uses blasts from underwater air guns. The sound waves from the air gun blasts are deflected by underground geologic strata and detected by sound wave receptors associated with the survey vessel. There are two types of surveys that can be performed: two dimension (2-D) and three dimension (3-D). 3-D surveys are the dominant and preferred exploration technique in the Gulf, although quite a few permits were issued during the study period for high resolution 2-D surveys. Most modern survey vessels tow multiple streamers (sound wave reception devices) such that for every linear mile traveled, they acquire data for a square mile of subsurface area (Brinkman 2002a, 2002b).

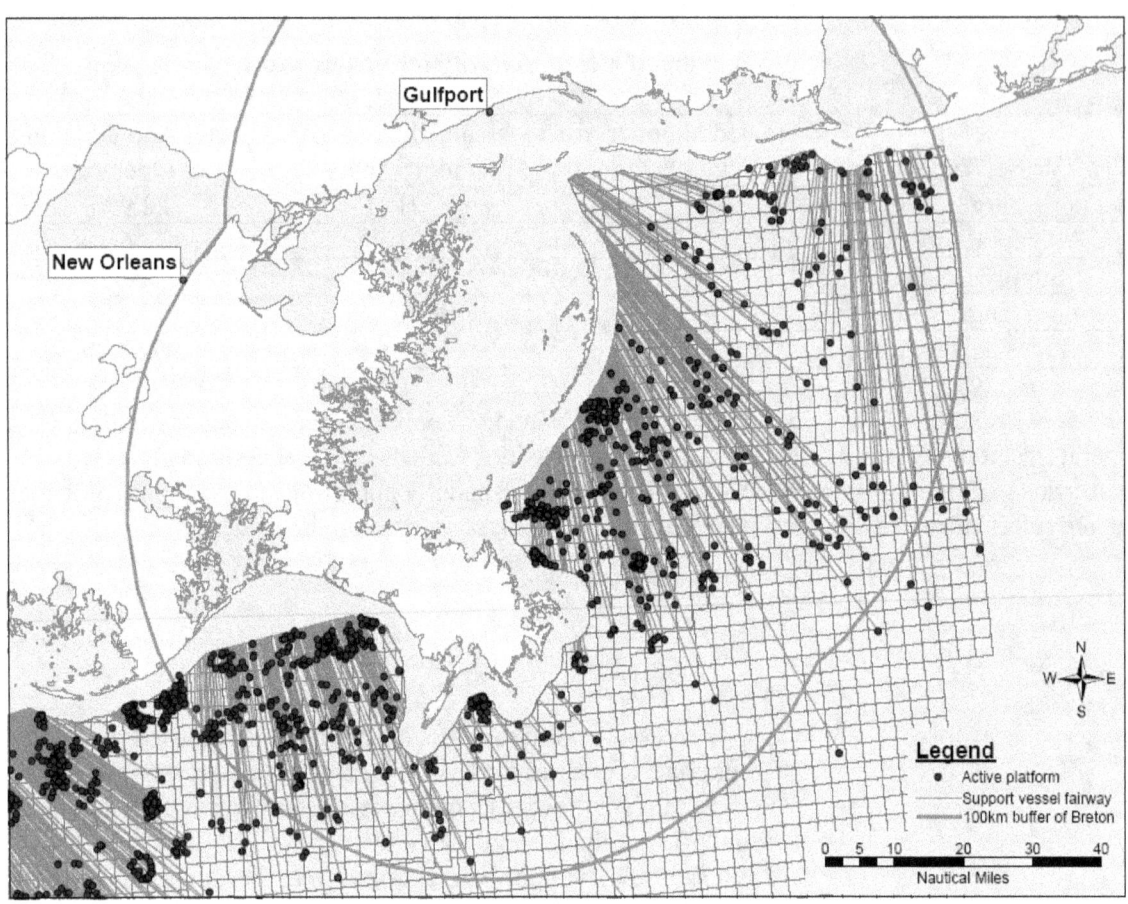

Figure 6-5. Location of Active Lease Blocks and Associated Support Vessel Fairways.

Survey vessel activity was provided by the Operation and Analysis Branch of the Engineering and Operations Division of MMS. Survey activities require a permit from MMS if the survey is intended for a block not currently under lease. Operators do not need to notify MMS if they intend to survey blocks they currently lease, such that the survey vessel activity used in this report underestimates actual activity. Due to issues of confidentiality, information about the location of permitted surveys could not be provided (Dellagiarino 2001). The Operation and Analysis Branch provided summary permit data for survey activities in these inactive lease blocks for 2000. It was assumed that activity levels for 2001 were similar to 2000, therefore the 2000 data were used to approximate 2001 activity. Given the small number of inactive lease blocks in the study area, the error associated with this assumption is believed to be relatively small.

The total hours of survey activity were estimated based on the total number of miles surveyed for 2-D surveys and total surface area surveyed for 3-D surveys. It was assumed that underway vessel speed for both 2-D and 3-D surveys is approximately 5 MPH (Brinkman 2002b).

Emissions associated with survey vessels are primarily from marine diesel engines used for propulsion and to provide electricity and compressed air to operate the survey equipment.

6-22

Emissions were estimated by applying the activity hours to marine engine emission factors. The emission factors used for this source category were based on emission equations included in support of the EPA's diesel marine vessel rule (U.S. EPA 2000). The EPA's emission factor equation uses operating load factors to generate emission factors in terms of kilowatt-hour (kW-hr), as noted in the equation below:

$$E \text{ (g/kW-hr)} = A \times (\text{Load Factors})^{-x} + B$$

where:

E is the power-based emission factor;

Constant A, intercept B, and exponent x were obtained from the U.S. EPA (2000) report.

For SO_2, it is necessary to first calculate Fuel Consumption using the following equation:

$$\text{Fuel Consumption (g/kW-hr)} = 14.12/(\text{fractional load}) + 205.717$$

It is assumed that diesel fuel, modeled after distillate fuel oil #2, is used in marine applications. Such fuel is assumed to have a sulfur content of 0.4%. This percentage of sulfur in the fuel should be multiplied by the Fuel Consumption calculated above, to estimate the Fuel Sulfur Flow as noted below:

$$\text{Fuel Sulfur Flow (g/kW-hr)} = \text{Fuel Consumption (g/kW-hr)} \times 0.004$$

The fuel sulfur flow is thus applied to the following equation to obtain a SO_2 emission rate:

$$SO_2 \text{ Emission Rate (g/kW-hr)} = A \times (\text{Fuel Sulfur Flow in g/kW-hr}) + B$$

where:

A and B are dimensionless constants provided in Table 5-1 of the U.S. EPA (2000) report. It should be noted that the A coefficient for the sulfur emission estimate was corrected in this study to 1.998 (which is rounded to 2.00), based on discussions with EPA staff concerning the correct value that should be used.

Horsepower and loading factor assumptions were obtained from the GMAQS (U.S. DOI, MMS 1995). The survey vessel emission factors used in the BNWA study are provided in Table 6-13 for 2-D seismic activities and Table 6-14 for seismic activities.

Table 6-13. Emission Factors for Survey Vessels - 2D Seismic.

Engines	Operating Load	Avg. HP	Avg. kW			
2	80%	776.00	578.66			
Pollutant	E (g/kW-hr)	Exponent (x)	Intercept (B)	Coefficient (A)	Kg/hr	lbs/hr
NO$_x$	10.62	1.50	10.45	0.13	6.15	13.55
SO$_2$*	1.78	N/A	0.00	2.00	1.03	2.27

*For SO$_2$ fuel sulfur flow (g/kW-hr) = 14.12/fractional load + 205.717 × fuel sulfur concentration
For this study the fuel sulfur concentration was assumed to be 0.4%

Table 6-14. Emission Factors for Survey Vessels - 3D Seismic.

Engines	Operating Load	Avg. HP	Avg. kW			
2	80%	776	578.66			
Pollutant	E (g/kW-hr)	Exponent (x)	Intercept (B)	Coefficient (A)	Kg/hr	lbs/hr
NO$_x$	10.62	1.50	10.45	0.13	6.15	13.55
SO$_2$*	1.78	N/A	0.00	2.00	1.03	2.27

*For SO$_2$ fuel sulfur flow (g/kW-hr) = 14.12/fractional load + 205.717 × fuel sulfur concentration
For this study the fuel sulfur concentration was assumed to be 0.4%

Hours of operation were estimated by adjusting the Gulfwide survey vessel hours of operation (Wilson et al. 2004) with the amount of unleased lease blocks associated with the BNWA. These estimates of survey vessel operations are summarized in Table 6-15. The hours of operation have also been adjusted to reflect the fact that survey vessels tend to have two engines for propulsion. It should also be noted that it is assumed that the amount of 2-D and 3-D vessel traffic in the Gulf were assumed to be proportional to the type of survey vessel traffic in the BNWA.

Table 6-15. Estimated Hours of Survey Vessel Operation in the BNWA.

Survey Vessel Type	Annual Hours of Operation
2-D	549
3-D	40
Total	589

The total hours of operation were applied to the EPA emission factor equation to estimate SO$_2$ and NO$_x$ emissions for the inactive lease blocks. Emissions were allocated to each inactive block based on the surface area of the lease block, as noted in the following equation.

$$E_{Si} = E_S \times (S_{ii}/S_{ti})$$

Where:

E_{Si}	=	Survey vessel emissions associated with lease block i
E_S	=	Total survey vessel emissions
S_{ii}	=	Surface area of inactive lease block i
S_{ti}	=	Total surface area of all inactive lease blocks

Only those survey vessel activities that occurred within the BNWA Study catchment area were included in this inventory of non-platform sources as noted in Figure 6-6.

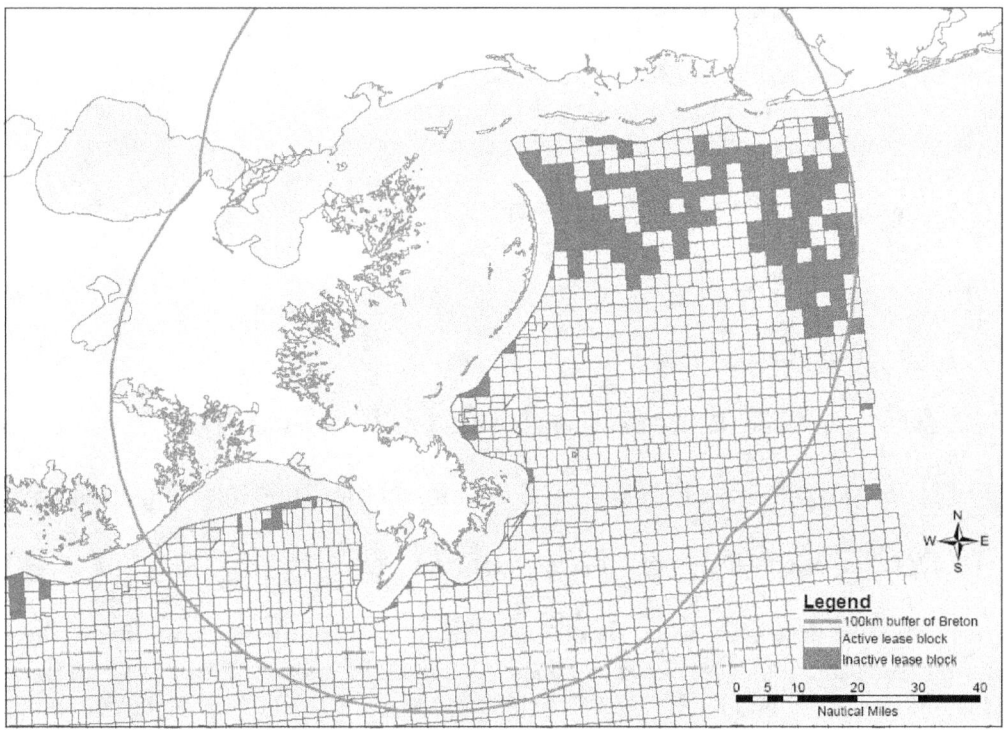

Figure 6-6. Location of Unleased Blocks.

6.2   NON-OCS OIL AND GAS PRODUCTION RELATED SOURCES

Non-OCS oil and gas production sources are vessels related to fishing, shipping of cargo and passengers, and military operations.

6.2.1 Commercial Fishing

The Gulf is an active commercial fishing area, providing a wide range of fish and seafood products. Detailed commercial fishing data were obtained from the National Oceanic & Atmospheric Administration's National Marine Fisheries Service (NMFS). Separate activity data were provided for the three different types of offshore fishing activities that occur in the Gulf: pelagic long line, reef, and shrimp fishing operations (Cramer 2001, Pattela 2001, Poffenberger, 2001). The activity data for these different fishing operations were provided as latitude and longitude for pelagic long line fishing operations and in terms of NMFS' statistical zones for reef and shrimp fishing. The associated activity data were extrapolated in to hours of opertion which were applied directly to emission factors to estimate emissions.

Emissions associated with commercial fishing vessels are attributed to the operation of diesel engines used for propulsion and other smaller diesel engines that are used to run generators or small cranes and winches to lift fish nets and lines onto the vessel. To estimate emissions from operating these diesel engines, the EPA's marine diesel emission equation (U.S. EPA 2000) was used. This EPA's emission factor equation uses operating load factors to generate emission factors in terms of kilowatt-hour (kW-hr), as noted in the equation below:

$$E \text{ (g/kW-hr)} = A \times \text{(Load Factors)}^{-x} + B$$

where:

E is the power-based emission factor;

Constant A, intercept B, and exponent x were obtained from the U.S. EPA (2000) report.

For SO_2, it is necessary to first calculate Fuel Consumption using the following equation:

$$\text{Fuel Consumption (g/kW-hr)} = 14.12/\text{(fractional load)} + 205.717$$

It is assumed that diesel fuel, modeled after distillate fuel oil #2, is used in marine applications. Such fuel is assumed to have a sulfur content of 0.4%. This percentage of sulfur in the fuel should be multiplied by the Fuel Consumption calculated above, to estimate the Fuel Sulfur Flow as noted below:

$$\text{Fuel Sulfur Flow (g/kW-hr)} = \text{Fuel Consumption (g/kW-hr)} \times 0.004$$

The fuel sulfur flow is thus applied to the following equation to obtain a SO_2 emission rate:

$$SO_2 \text{ Emission Rate (g/kW-hr)} = A \times \text{(Fuel Sulfur Flow in g/kW-hr)} + B$$
where:

A and B are dimensionless constants provided in Table 5-1 of the U.S. EPA (2000) report and noted in Table 6-16 below.

Assumptions about fishing vessel horsepower and typical load factors were provided in the GMAQS (U.S. DOI, MMS 1995). This information was applied to the EPA emission factor equation deriving the emission factors that are noted in Table 6-16.

Table 6-16. Commercial Fishing Emission Factors.

Pollutant	E (g/kW-hr)	Exponent (x)	Intercept (B)	Coefficient (A)	Average kW rating	kg/hr	lbs/hr
NO_x	10.62	1.50	10.45	0.13	223.71	2.38	5.23
SO_2*	1.78	N/A	0.00	2.00	223.71	0.40	0.88

Assuming operating load is 80% (U.S. EPA 2000)
From GMAQS, diesel range from 100 to 500 hp average assumed to be 300 hp = 223.71 kW
*For SO_2 fuel sulfur flow (g/kW-hr) = 14.12/fractional load + 205.717 × fuel sulfur concentration. For this study the fuel sulfur concentration was assumed to be 0.4%

These emission factors were applied to the hours of operation provided by the NMFS to calculate emissions for this source category (see Tables 6-17 and 6-18). Commercial fishing locations were also provided by the NMFS. Reef and shrimp fishing operations are delineated by NMFS statistical zones. For line fishing operations, operating hours were estimated based on the assumption that it takes approximately 24 hours to tend each set. NMFS provided latitude and longitude coordinates for line fishing operations. Emissions were spatially allocated for these three activities by overlaying a GIS plot of MMS lease blocks onto the NMFS data and extracted the data associated with lease blocks within 100 km of the BNWA.

Table 6-17. Commercial Fishing Vessel Activity Data.

NMFS Zone	Operations (hours)	
	Shrimp	Reef
10	6,406.26	18,693.40
11	20,853.21	15,772.00
12	10,201.30	2,732.00
13	36,869.06	15,514.50
Total	74,329.82	52,711.90

Table 6-18. Line Fishing Activity Data.

Latitude	Longitude	Projection ID	Block ID	Sets	Operations (hours)
28.55	-89.28	NH16-10	410	1	24
28.55	-89.2	NH16-10	411	1	24
28.55	-89.13	NH16-10	413	1	24
28.57	-89.12	NH16-10	413	4	96
28.57	-89.43	NH16-10	363	1	24
28.53	-89.1	NH16-10	414	1	24
28.57	-89.08	NH16-10	414	1	24
28.58	-89.47	NH16-10	362	1	24
28.58	-89.38	NH16-10	364	1	24
28.62	-89.43	LA9A	95	1	24
28.58	-89.15	NH16-10	369	1	24
28.62	-89.35	NH16-10	320	1	24
28.6	-89.07	NH16-10	370	1	24
28.6	-89.03	NH16-10	371	1	24
28.6	-89	NH16-10	372	3	72
28.58	-88.93	NH16-10	373	1	24
28.6	-88.88	NH16-10	374	1	24
28.62	-88.9	NH16-10	374	1	24
28.62	-88.83	NH16-10	375	1	24
28.65	-89.32	NH16-10	321	1	24
28.58	-88.8	NH16-10	376	1	24
28.62	-88.78	NH16-10	376	1	24
28.62	-89.17	NH16-10	324	1	24
28.65	-89.12	NH16-10	325	1	24
28.65	-89.07	NH16-10	326	1	24
28.67	-89.75	LA8A	139	1	24
28.63	-89.03	NH16-10	327	1	24
28.65	-89.03	NH16-10	327	1	24
28.63	-89	NH16-10	328	2	48
28.62	-88.95	NH16-10	329	1	24
28.65	-88.93	NH16-10	329	1	24
28.63	-88.87	NH16-10	330	1	24
28.65	-88.85	NH16-10	331	1	24
28.63	-88.77	NH16-10	332	1	24
28.7	-89.22	NH16-10	279	1	24
28.63	-88.67	NH16-10	334	1	24
28.67	-89.1	NH16-10	282	1	24
28.68	-88.93	NH16-10	285	1	24
28.68	-88.95	NH16-10	285	1	24
28.7	-88.93	NH16-10	285	1	24
28.68	-88.85	NH16-10	287	1	24
28.7	-88.72	NH16-10	289	1	24
28.7	-88.75	NH16-10	289	1	24

Table 6-18. Line Fishing Activity Data (Continued).

Latitude	Longitude	Projection ID	Block ID	Sets	Operations (hours)
28.67	-88.65	NH16-10	291	1	24
28.68	-88.6	NH16-10	292	1	24
28.73	-88.97	NH16-10	240	1	24
28.72	-88.82	NH16-10	243	1	24
28.73	-88.82	NH16-10	243	1	24
28.73	-88.83	NH16-10	243	1	24
28.75	-88.85	NH16-10	243	1	24
28.73	-88.8	NH16-10	244	1	24
28.75	-88.8	NH16-10	244	1	24
28.75	-89.25	NH16-10	191	1	24
28.73	-88.7	NH16-10	246	1	24
28.78	-88.85	NH16-10	199	1	24
28.78	-88.77	NH16-10	200	1	24
28.78	-88.75	NH16-10	201	1	24
28.78	-88.7	NH16-10	202	1	24
28.82	-88.92	NH16-10	153	3	72
28.82	-88.95	NH16-10	153	1	24
28.82	-88.9	NH16-10	154	1	24
28.83	-88.83	NH16-10	155	1	24
28.83	-88.85	NH16-10	155	1	24
28.83	-88.8	NH16-10	156	1	24
28.8	-88.67	NH16-10	158	1	24
28.82	-88.68	NH16-10	158	2	48
28.82	-88.65	NH16-10	159	1	24
28.83	-88.53	NH16-10	161	1	24
28.83	-88.55	NH16-10	161	2	48
28.83	-88.5	NH16-10	162	1	24
28.85	-88.97	NH16-10	108	1	24
28.85	-88.9	NH16-10	110	1	24
28.85	-88.62	NH16-10	115	1	24
28.88	-88.65	NH16-10	115	1	24
28.88	-88.6	NH16-10	116	1	24
28.85	-88.48	NH16-10	118	1	24
28.85	-88.38	NH16-10	120	1	24
28.87	-88.32	NH16-10	121	2	48
28.92	-88.58	NH16-10	72	1	24
28.9	-88.52	NH16-10	73	1	24
28.9	-88.55	NH16-10	73	1	24
28.97	-88.78	NH16-10	24	1	24
29.02	-89.7	LA8	63	1	24
28.95	-88.35	NH16-10	33	1	24
29.08	-89.85	LA8	38	1	24
29.07	-89.75	LA8	41	1	24

Table 6-18. Line Fishing Activity Data (Continued).

Latitude	Longitude	Projection ID	Block ID	Sets	Operations (hours)
29.08	-88.35	NH16-07	907	1	24
29.1	-88.25	NH16-07	909	1	24
29.13	-88.37	NH16-07	862	1	24
29.13	-88.28	NH16-07	864	2	48
29.13	-88.25	NH16-07	865	1	24
29.15	-88.22	NH16-07	865	1	24
29.17	-88.07	NH16-07	825	1	24
29.2	-88.05	NH16-07	781	1	24
29.28	-88.3	LA10A	278	1	24
29.35	-88.43	LA10A	268	1	24
29.35	-88.38	LA10A	267	1	24
29.35	-88.3	LA10A	265	1	24
29.38	-88.23	LA10A	244	1	24
29.37	-88.22	LA10A	245	1	24
29.37	-88.15	LA10A	246	1	24
29.38	-88.12	LA10A	247	1	24
29.38	-88.05	LA10A	248	4	96
29.42	-88.25	LA10A	229	1	24
29.95	-87.98	NH16-07	34	1	24
				Total hours of operation	2,880

Because the location of the fishing areas does not generally change from year to year, it was considered reasonable to assume that 2001 activity would be similar to 2000 activity. Thus, the base year 2000 emissions that are apportioned to the five statistical zones (i.e., zones 10, 11, 12, 13, and 14) near the BNWA were used to represent 2001 emissions (Figure 6-7). Commercial fishing emission estimates for reef and shrimp fishing operations were spatially allocated using the following formula:

$$E_{CFi} = E_{CFz} \times (S_i / S_{CFz})$$

where:

E_{CFi} = Commercial fishing emissions for lease block i
E_{CFz} = Commercial fishing emissions for NMFS area z
S_i = Surface area of lease block i
S_{CFz} = Total surface area of NMFS area z

Where a lease block was included in two NMFS areas, the assignment was made proportional to the area of the NMFS zone that the lease block occupied. For example, lease block AB is split between NMFS zones 12 and 13. Seventy five percent of lease block AB is included in zone 12 and 25% of lease block AB is in zone 13. In this example, emissions associated with NMFS zones 12 and 13 would be split in lease block AB, proportional to the area with which each zone is associated.

Line fishing emissions were assigned to individual lease blocks based on the latitude and longitude coordinates provided by NMFS and the estimated hours of operation.

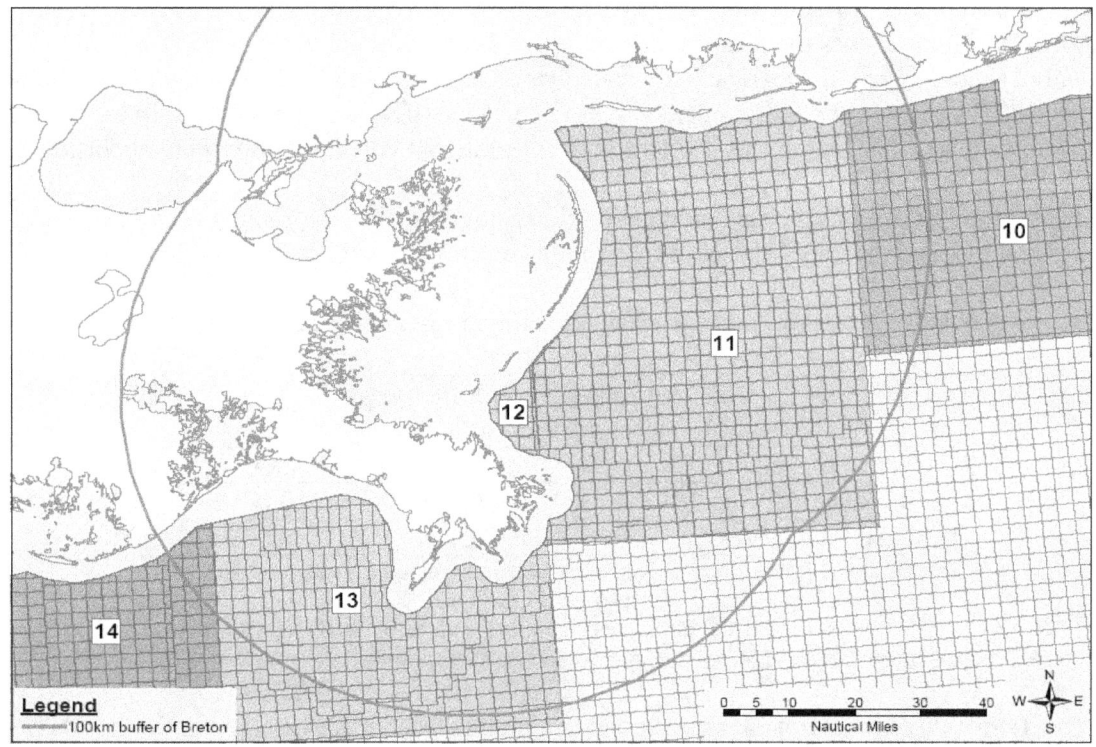

Figure 6-7. NMFS Fishing Zones with Lease Blocks.

With regard to recreational fishing, it was decided that the majority of recreational fishing occurs within state waters, and therefore this source category was not included in this inventory. It is recognized that some small portion of recreational fishing occurs near platforms that are not in state waters. Unfortunately, data could not be identified to quantify recreational fishing near oil platforms.

6.2.2 Commercial Marine Vessels

Commercial marine vessels (CMVs) are involved in transporting a wide range of agricultural, manufacturing, and chemical products through the Gulf. CMVs tend to be powered by either diesel engines that combust diesel or residual oil fuels or steam ships that burn residual fuel. Though some emissions may occur due to evaporative losses of volatile chemical products, most of the emissions associated with CMVs are from the combustion of the fuels used to propel the vessels.

6-31

CMV emission estimates for diesel and residual powered vessels were developed using ton-mileage emission factors the EPA's National Emission Inventory (NEI) database (U.S. EPA 2003) shown in Table 6-19, and ship-lane activity data obtained from the Army Corps of Engineers. Steamship emission estimates were also extrapolated from the EPA's NEI (U.S. EPA 2003). Note, the approach used to develop the CMV emission factors accounts for the relative size of the diesel and residual fleets, and allows for application of the emission factors to the total ton-mile data reported by the Army Corps of Engineers. The BNWA study area includes several significant shipping lanes that originate at the Mississippi River and head east toward the Atlantic, south to Central America, and west toward Corpus Christi. The shipping lanes included in the BNWA account for approximately 40% (i.e, 1.45×10^6 ton-miles) of the ship traffic in the Federal waters of the Central and Western portions of the GOM. Emissions were apportioned to individual lease blocks by mapping the GIS shipping data set onto MMS lease block shape files and apportioning emissions based on the ton mileage of each link. Emissions associated for individual links within a lease block were summed to estimate total emissions for the lease block.

Table 6-19. Cargo Traffic Emission Factors for Commercial Marine Vessels.

Emission Factor (g/ton-nautical mile)*		
Pollutant	NO_x	SO_2**
Diesel Powered Vessels	0.4727	0.0792
Residual Fueled Vessels	0.0121	0.0090

*The emission factors are weighted for total gross ton mileage as such data are generally not disaggregated by vessel fuel type
**For this study the fuel sulfur concentration for diesel powered vessels was assumed to be 0.4%, and for residual powered vessels was assumed to be 2.7%

Only those commercial marine vessel shipping lanes that are located within the BNWA inventory catchment area were included in this inventory of non-platform sources. These shipping lanes are noted in Figure 6-8.

6.2.3 Military Vessel Operations

The U.S. Navy and Coast Guard frequently patrol and have maneuvers in the Gulf. The U.S. military vessel fleet consists of vessels powered by a variety of engines including older residual fueled steam turbines, marine diesel engines, and high speed diesel turbines.

Contacts were made with the Navy to obtain activity data necessary to estimate vessel emissions. Despite these repeated data requests and promises by the Navy to provide the required data, no data were ever submitted. Therefore, the data the Navy provided for the GMAQS (U.S. DOI, MMS 1995) were used in this inventory. It was assumed that naval vessel activity remained constant during this period and no adjustments were made to the activity data. Hours of operation for each vessel were assumed to be 24 hours per day, 365 days per year.

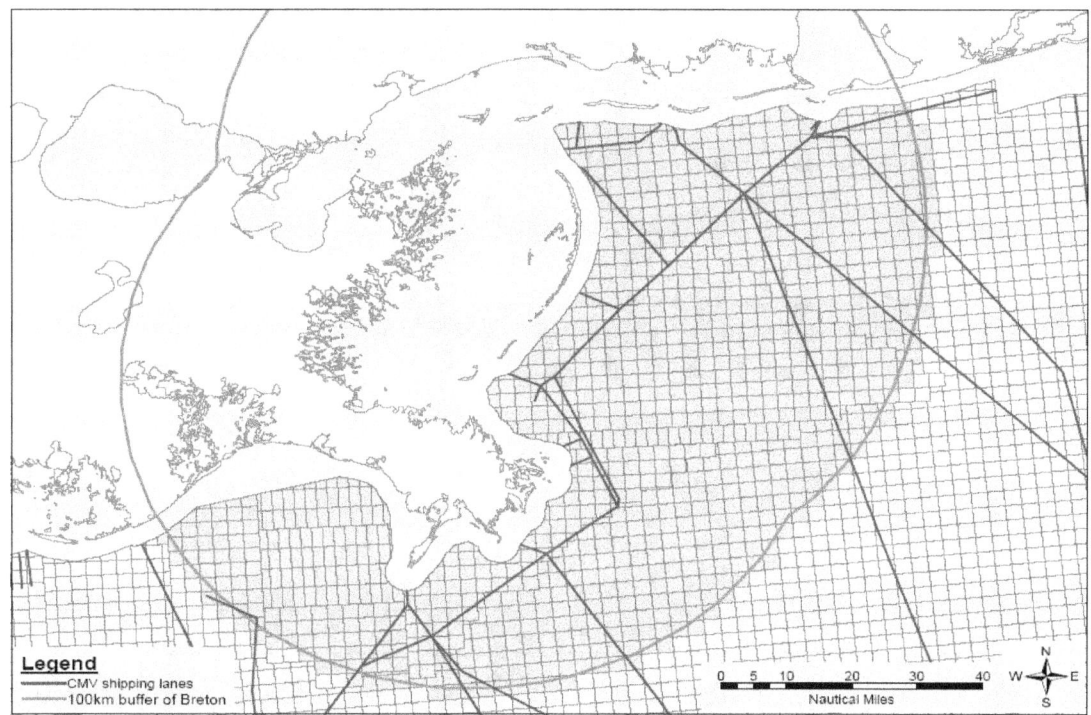

Figure 6-8. Commercial Marine Vessel Shipping Lanes and Lease Blocks.

Navy vessel emission estimates were developed for marine diesel engines using the EPA marine diesel equations. The EPA's emission factor equation uses operating load factors and vessel horsepower rating to generate emission factors in terms of kilowatt-hour (kW-hr), as noted in the equation below. A load factor of 80% was assumed and engine horsepower for each vessel was obtained in the GMAQS (U.S. DOI, MMS 1995).

E (g/kW-hr) = A $\times$ (Load Factors)$^{-x}$ +B

where:

E is the power-based emission factor;

Constant A, intercept B, and exponent x were obtained from the U.S. EPA (2000) report.

For SO_2, it is necessary to first calculate Fuel Consumption using the following equation:

Fuel Consumption (g/kW-hr) = 14.12/(fractional load) + 205.717

It is assumed that diesel fuel, modeled after distillate fuel oil #2, is used in marine applications. Such fuel is assumed to have a sulfur content of 0.4%. This percentage of sulfur in the fuel should be multiplied by the Fuel Consumption calculated above, to estimate the Fuel Sulfur Flow as noted below:

Fuel Sulfur Flow (g/kW-hr) = Fuel Consumption (g/kW-hr) × 0.004

The fuel sulfur flow is thus applied to the following equation to obtain a SO_2 emission rate:

SO_2 Emission Rate (g/kW-hr) = A × (Fuel Sulfur Flow in g/kW-hr) + B

where:

A and B are dimensionless constants provided in Table 5-1 of the U.S. EPA (2000) report and are noted in Table 6-20.

The diesel Naval emission factors used in the Breton Inventory are noted in Table 6-20.

Table 6-20. Diesel Naval Vessel Emission Factors.

Pollutant	E (g/kW-hr)	Exponent (x)	Intercept (B)	Coefficient (A)	Avg kW rating	Kg/hr	lbs/hr
Naval Vessel: MSO							
NO_x	10.62	1.50	10.45	0.13	428.78	4.56	10.04
SO_2*	1.78	N/A	0.00	2.00	428.78	0.76	1.68
Naval Vessel: MCM							
NO_x	10.62	1.5	10.4496	0.1255	447.4	4.75	10.48
SO_2*	1.78	N/A	0	1.998	447.4	0.80	1.76
Naval Vessel: PHM							
NO_x	10.62	1.5	10.4496	0.1255	596.6	6.34	13.97
SO_2*	1.78	N/A	0	1.998	596.6	1.06	2.34
Naval Vessel: TAG							
NO_x	10.62	1.50	10.45	0.13	1,043.98	11.09	24.45
SO_2*	1.78	N/A	0.00	2.00	1,043.98	1.86	4.10
Naval Vessel: TAGS(50)							
NO_x	10.62	1.50	10.45	0.13	1,864.25	19.81	43.67
SO_2*	1.78	N/A	0.00	2.00	1,864.25	3.32	7.32
Naval Vessel: LSD							
NO_x	10.62	1.50	10.45	0.13	7,643.43	81.21	179.04
SO_2*	1.78	N/A	0.00	2.00	7,643.43	13.61	30.01
Naval Vessel: TAGS(40)							
NO_x	10.62	1.50	10.45	0.13	8,948.40	95.08	209.61
SO_2*	1.78	N/A	0.00	2.00	8,948.40	15.94	35.13

Table 6-20. Diesel Naval Vessel Emission Factors (Continued).

Pollutant	E (g/kW-hr)	Exponent (x)	Intercept (B)	Coefficient (A)	Avg kW rating	Kg/hr	lbs/hr
Naval Vessel: TAK(II)							
NO_x	10.62	1.50	10.45	0.13	10,066.95	106.96	235.81
SO_2*	1.78	N/A	0.00	2.00	10,066.95	17.93	39.52

*For SO_2 fuel sulfur flow (g/kW-hr) = 14.12/fractional load + 205.717 × fuel sulfur concentration. For this study the fuel sulfur concentration was assumed to be 0.4%

Steamship and diesel turbine engine vessel emission estimates were determined differently. Fuel consumption data for these vessel types were supplied by the Navy in the GMAQS (U.S. DOI, MMS 1995). Emissions factors for residual oil-fueled steamship vessels were obtained from the EPA's *Documentation for Aircraft, Commercial Marine Vessel, Locomotive, and other Nonroad Components of the National Emission Inventory* (U.S. EPA 2003). For turbine-powered vessels, updated emission factors were obtained from the EPA's *AP-42* (U.S. EPA 2002). These fuel based emission factors for residual fuel steamships and vessels equipped with diesel turbine engines are noted in Table 6-21.

Table 6-21. Steamship Emission Factors.

Pollutant	Emission Factor (lbs/1000L)	
	Residual fueled steamship	Diesel Turbine
NO_x	14.38	32.19
SO_2	85.90	14.78

Source: U.S. EPA 2003

The Coast Guard provided data that included the number of vessels operating in the Gulf, the type of vessel, the number of engines, and horsepower of each engine, the total number of operating hours for each, and the percentage of time each vessel spent in the OCS (McClellan 2002, Peschke 2002, Thomas 2001). From this data, the total number of operating hours was calculated for each type of boat.

To estimate emissions from the marine diesel engines, the EPA's marine diesel engine emission factor equations were used. This emission factor equation uses operating load factors to generate emission factors in terms of kilowatt-hour (kW-hr), as noted in the equation below:

$$E \text{ (g/kW-hr)} = A \times (\text{Load Factors})^{-x} + B$$

where:

E is the power-based emission factor;

Constant A, intercept B, and exponent x were obtained from the U.S. EPA (2000) report.

For SO_2, it is necessary to first calculate Fuel Consumption using the following equation:

Fuel Consumption (g/kW-hr) = 14.12/(fractional load) + 205.717

It is assumed that diesel fuel, modeled after distillate fuel oil #2, is used in marine applications. Such fuel is assumed to have a sulfur content of 0.4%. This percentage of sulfur in the fuel was multiplied by the Fuel Consumption calculated above, to estimate the Fuel Sulfur Flow as noted below:

Fuel Sulfur Flow (g/kW-hr) = Fuel Consumption (g/kW-hr) × 0.004

The fuel sulfur flow was applied to the following equation to obtain a SO_2 emission rate:

SO_2 Emission Rate (g/kW-hr) = A × (Fuel Sulfur Flow in g/kW-hr) + B

where:

A and B are dimensionless constants provided in Table 5-1 of the U.S. EPA (2000) report and included in Table 6-22.

Assuming a load factor of 80%, and using the provided horsepower data, emission factors were derived using the above equations; these emission factors are noted in Table 6-22. Emissions from each vessel type were calculated and totaled to estimate emissions for all Coast Guard vessels operating in the Gulf.

Table 6-22. Emission Factors for Coast Guard Vessels.

Pollutant	E (g/kW-hr)	Exponent (x)	Intercept (B)	Coefficient (A)	Avg kw rating	Kg/hr	lbs/hr
87-Foot Coast Guard Vessels							
NO_x	10.62	1.50	10.45	0.13	1,099.91	11.69	25.76
SO_2*	1.78	N/A	0.00	2.00	1,099.91	1.96	4.32
110-Foot Coast Guard Vessels							
NO_x	10.62	1.50	10.45	0.13	5,070.76	53.88	118.78
SO_2*	1.78	N/A	0.00	2.00	5,070.76	9.03	19.91
175-Foot Coast Guard Vessels							
NO_x	10.62	1.50	10.45	0.13	1,267.69	13.47	29.69
SO_2*	1.78	N/A	0.00	2.00	1,267.69	2.26	4.98

*For SO_2 fuel sulfur flow (g/kW-hr) = 14.12/fractional load + 205.717 × fuel sulfur concentration. For this study the fuel sulfur concentration was assumed to be 0.4%

It is assumed that the composition of the Coast Guard's Gulf fleet and operations have not significantly changed in 2001; therefore the 2000 estimates were used to represent 2001 activity.

All military activity data and emissions were estimated Gulfwide, and were allocated equally throughout the Federal waters of the Gulf (Eastern, Central and Western Gulf areas), as noted in the equation below. This allocation was made based on the surface area of the lease blocks.

$$E_{MVi} = E_{MV} \times (S_i/S_{TNG})$$

where:

E_{MVi}	=	Military vessel emissions associated with lease block i
E_{MV}	=	Total military vessel emissions for total Northern Gulf area
S_i	=	Surface area of lease block i
S_{TNG}	=	Surface area of total Northern Gulf lease blocks

Only those military vessel activities that occurred within the BNWA Study catchment area were included in this inventory.

7. RESULTS

7.1   SUMMARY OF STUDY APPROACH

MMS' *Data Quality Control and Emissions Inventories of OCS Oil and Gas Production Activities in the Breton Area of the Gulf of Mexico* required an extensive inventory development effort. The study includes all oil and gas production platforms and non-platform sources within 100 km of the BNWA. Pollutants covered in the inventory are SO_2 and NO_x.

MMS attempted to collect activity data from each and every active offshore oil production platform in the vicinity of the BNWA. Operators were provided with the BOADS Visual Basic activity data collection software for compiling monthly data from August 2000 through September 2001. Nearly 600 oil and gas production platforms submitted monthly equipment activity data files. The platform equipment surveyed includes:

- Amine units;
- Boilers/heaters/burners;
- Diesel engines;
- Drilling equipment;
- Flares;
- Natural gas engines; and
- Natural gas turbines.

Non-platform sources covered in the inventory are:

- Commercial fishing;
- Commercial marine vessels;
- Drilling rigs;
- Military vessel operations;
- Pipelaying operations;
- Platform construction and removal vessels;
- Support helicopters;
- Support vessels; and
- Survey vessels.

Rigorous QC was performed on the activity data collected from platform operators. Tasks were implemented to correct the number of operating hours provided for a given month, fill in missing monthly operating data (if equipment was operational), verify and correct activity values such as fuel heating value, make sure that the equipment shown to be flared included a flare ID and activity record, fill in missing stack parameters with surrogates, and double check exit velocity and fuel usage totals by recalculating the parameters. The monthly activity data collected from the platform operators were then combined with emission factors and algorithms to develop the platform emission estimates.

Inventory data files were compiled with the oil and gas production platform data, suitable for use in air quality modeling applications. In addition to monthly emission estimates by pollutant and individual piece of equipment, the files include the company, structure, and complex ID, lease number, block and area number, and latitude/longitude. For each piece of equipment, stack parameter information such as outlet height, exit velocity, and exit temperature is also presented.

ERG also compiled activity data and developed emission estimates for non-platform sources within the vicinity of the BNWA. For the most part, the emission factors used to calculate the emissions from all of the engines for these sources were obtained from the EPA's OTAQ in Ann Arbor, Michigan. OTAQ published the emission equations along with their Diesel Marine Vessel Rule in 2002. The resulting emission estimates are disaggregated to MMS lease blocks.

7.2   PRESENTION OF ANNUAL EMISSION ESTIMATES

The platform and non-platform emission estimates are presented in Tables 7-1 through 7-3. Table 7-1 summarizes the total platform emission estimates, Table 7-2 summarizes the total non-platform emission estimates, and Table 7-3 presents the combined platform and non-platform estimates.

7.3   LIMITATIONS

As with the development of any inventory of activity data or emission estimates, the accuracy can vary considerably depending upon the accuracy of the activity data obtained and the emission factors used. The key limitation and source of uncertainty associated with OCS oil/gas production platform inventory effort pertains to platform ownership changes that make it difficult to track month-to-month completeness. At the equipment level, there is no way of knowing how well the operators understood what activity data were being requested. This lack of understanding is particularly of concern for flares. The emission estimates for flares are directly dependent upon the accuracy of the activity data provided by the operators. While this is true for all of the equipment in this inventory, there is a higher chance of operators misinterpreting the data requested for flares.

In addition, some emission estimates were developed based on the use of surrogates if the actual data needed to estimate emissions were not provided directly. This introduces uncertainty because the data may have been omitted intentionally by the operator, but extraneous data were provided that should have been omitted as well. Uncertainty is introduced when the survey respondent lacks an understanding of the data request or incorrectly interprets the data request, and when conflicting survey data are reviewed and adjusted for use in developing emission estimates. Typographical data entry errors also probably occurred in the monthly activity data that were not identified during the QA/QC process.

This project included the development of two software programs; the BOADS software to gather OCS oil and gas production platform activity data, and the DBMS software to calculate air emissions based on this activity data and current emission factors. In a recent review of the draft GOADS 2000 inventory (Wilson et al. 2004), a discrepancy was noticed between reported BOADS and GOADS venting and flaring activity data and the vented and flared gas volumes reported on the Oil and Gas Operations Report (OGOR), Form MMS-4054. Based on an extensive quality control of records for several platforms, the BOADS software used to collect activity data was adjusted to improve flaring and venting volume estimates in the BOADS inventory. The adjustments to the software resulted in considerably more accurate accounting of flaring and venting volumes, and volumes closer to the OGOR values. The emissions from these sources in the BOADS inventory may still be higher than actual values, however. MMS has made several modifications to the GOADS software to reduce these errors in the future. The software has been modified to simplify the data requested each month to only the equipment variables that change monthly. This will reduce data entry volume, processing time, and the likelihood of data entry errors.

The estimates for some non-platform source categories such as support vessels and naval operations were based on adjustments made to activity data that were included in the GMAQS (U.S. DOI, MMS 1995). Much of the non-platform activity data used in the 1995 study were derived from a 1992 Survey of Offshore Operators undertaken by the Offshore Operators Committee (OOC). This 1992 report contains useful information, and it would have been helpful if a similar study could have been performed for this 2000-2001 inventory effort.

In addition, most of the non-platform sources are powered by marine diesel engines. In this study, marine diesel emission factors were developed using recent EPA emission equations derived from a large number of "in use" vessel test data. These emission equations require horsepower and operating load factors. Typical horsepower and load factors were obtained from the GMAQS (U.S. DOI, MMS 1995). These values are averages, such that actual emissions from specific vessels may be significantly different. These averages lend uncertainty to the estimates for drill ships and pipelaying operations, among others. It should also be noted that the activity data used to estimate emissions from survey vessels were only for surveys implemented at non-active lease blocks. Survey activity for active lease blocks is considered confidential and not tracked by MMS; therefore actual BNWA survey vessel activity will be larger than the activity quantified in this inventory.

7.4 RECOMMENDATIONS

Based on the limitations discussed above, recommendations for future inventory efforts for platform sources in vicinity of the BNWA focus on the data gathering tools used. The uncertainty associated with the flare emission estimates is due to the interpretation of the data requested by the operators as well as the pre-processing steps applied prior to development of the emission estimates. Plans are already in place to improve the data collection software for this equipment type. In addition, an overall improvement will be made to the software to simplify the data requested each month to only the equipment variables that change monthly. This will reduce data entry volume, processing time, and the likelihood of data entry errors.

Improvements in the data collection software, continued operator education and training, use of the MMS web site to post Frequently Asked Questions (FAQs), and increased efforts to identify companies that need to respond to the data request will reduce much of the uncertainty associated with future inventory efforts.

For non-platform sources, the following recommendations are provided to improve the accuracy of the emission estimates or enhance the spatial allocation of the estimates. These suggestions are provided by source category in order of significance relative to total emissions.

- **Implementation of Support Vessels Survey** - Implementation of a survey of marine vessels supporting offshore oil platforms can provide important data that would allow for the development of a more accurate estimate of emissions from these vessels. This support vessel survey could collect detailed information about vessel size, horsepower rating, and typical operating loads, as well as annual, seasonal, and daily activity. This information could be used to update the OOC's survey performed in 1992 for the GMAQS. The new survey vessel inventory could be used to develop emission estimates in terms that can be readily applied to state-of-the-art GIS tools to spatially allocate emissions with greater accuracy.

- **Development of Drill Ship Database** - Currently, MMS collects very specific data on where specific drill ships operate and the length of time they spend at a given site. In the BNWA inventory, the average horsepower and load data were used to estimate emissions from these sources. Some vessels may be significantly larger or smaller than these average values, such that actual emissions may differ significantly from the estimated emissions. A drill ship database could contain information about vessel size, the number and horsepower of primary propulsion engines and ancillary engines, and better estimates on typical operating loads. This database could be linked with MMS' drill ship-specific activity data and available emission factors to provide more accurate emission estimates.

- **Implementation of Pipelaying Survey** – MMS maintains an excellent GIS file of pipelaying construction and maintenance activities which is very useful in assigning emissions to appropriate lease blocks. The emission estimates that have been developed for the BNWA inventory for this source category are based on many assumptions that were carried over from the GMAQS, particularly regarding the number of vessels needed for pipeline construction and maintenance and the horsepower rating and typical load of the primary propulsion and ancillary engines. Emission estimates can be improved by updating these assumptions through interviews with companies involved in these activities.

- **Platform Construction and Removal Vessels** – The current approach to estimating emissions associated with the construction and removal of offshore oil platforms is based on the number of pilings that a platform has and the ocean depth at the platform. These data are not readily available, and the data set developed for this source category in the BNWA inventory is not complete. Approximately 20% of the data do not include the number of platform pilings; for these cases, a surrogate was developed that is based on the number of floors associated with a given platform. There is also a concern that piling drilling associated with platform construction is not included in the emission estimates. An emission estimation approach needs to be developed to account for drilling associated with platform construction, or to determine if the drilling emissions are already associated with the drill ships category. It is important to insure that these drilling estimates do not double count with emission estimates for the drill ship source category. There is a similar concern of double counting with support vessels that may be involved with the construction or removal of platforms. To resolve these issues, it will be necessary to study this source category more fully and meet with staff from companies involved with these activities.

- **Implementation of Survey Vessel Survey** - MMS maintains excellent records of survey vessel activity; the problem is that these records are only required for non-active lease blocks. Survey activities related to active lease blocks are considered confidential information and are not tracked by MMS. It should be pointed out that there are a relatively small number of survey vessels operating in the entire Gulf. In order to develop an estimate of survey activities associated with active lease blocks, it is necessary to survey the companies that provide geophysical surveying services to estimate annual operating hours (excluding activities in the Eastern Gulf area, state, and international waters) and typical operating loads to develop a BNWA estimate for this source category. Survey vessel activity and emissions associated with the non-active lease blocks can be removed from the BNWA estimate to approximate emissions in the active lease blocks. These emissions can be applied equally to the active lease blocks based on a surrogate, such as surface area, in order to maintain the confidentiality of these data, while still providing complete emission estimates for this source category.

- **Development of Military Vessel Database** - As noted in this report, obtaining detailed data from the military can sometimes be very difficult. In the current inventory, emission estimates for the Navy are based on conservative estimates of the amount of time vessels operate in the vicinity of the BNWA; actual emissions may be significantly lower than these estimates. Unfortunately, the Navy did not provide any additional information to adjust these estimates to more accurately reflect actual emissions. It is recommended that a database be developed with all of the data required to estimate emissions and spatially and temporally adjust these estimates to represent activity in the vicinity of the BNWA. The database could include assumptions about the current vessel fleet operating in the Gulf, the horsepower of the primary and ancillary engines of each vessel, typical operating loads, and estimates of seasonal and annual hours of operation, as well as information concerning the geographic area where these vessels typically operate. This database could be shared with the Navy and Coast Guard, and they hopefully would update it with their own, more accurate data and submit it to MMS for inclusion in the BNWA inventory.

- **Implementation of Support Helicopter Survey** - As with support vessels, implementation of a detailed survey of support helicopters that service offshore oil platforms would allow for better quantification of the types of helicopters currently used, a better estimate of the hours of operation, as well as information to help spatially distribute estimated emissions. The data obtained from such a study should be compiled in a format compatible with GIS data files associated with the current inventory.

7.5   COMPARISON WITH OTHER STUDIES

At the completion of any emissions inventory effort, one final, useful QA/QC check is to compare the inventory results with those from similar inventories. The most applicable inventory to use in a comparison is presented in the MMS report, *Emission Inventories of OCS Production and Development Activities in the Gulf Of Mexico* (Coe et al. 2003). The report contains base year 2000 (January-December) emission estimates for all sources within 100 km of the BNWA.

Table 7-4 compares some of the daily platform emission estimates for OCS oil and gas production platforms presented in Coe et al. (2003) with those developed in this study.

The primary source of NO_X in both studies is natural gas engines. The number of natural gas engines (NGEs) in the two studies is similar (513 units in this study, 499 in the base year 2000 study). Aside from the reported activity data for each equipment type, a review of the emission factors used in each study provides a good indication of why the NO_X emission -estimates are lower in the current study. The estimates in both studies were developed using *AP-42* emission factors (U.S. EPA 2002), but the emission factors have been changed for natural gas engines. On average, the NO_x emission factors for natural gas engines are 50% lower than the factors applied in Coe et al. (2003). The contribution of natural gas engines to total NO_x emissions accounts for a large portion (84%) of the emissions reported in the base year 2000 study.

The discrepancy in the SO_2 emission estimates is due to the flare estimates in the two studies. In the base year 2000 study, 67% of the SO_2 emissions are from flares. Again, the number of units in the two studies is similar (data reported for 45 flares in the current study, vs. 51 flares in the base year 2000 study). In the current study, flares account for less than 1% of total SO_2 emissions. In developing the final Breton DBMS, a calculation error was corrected for the current study.

Table 7-1. Total Platform Emission Estimates.

Equipment	NO_x Emissions (tpy)	SO_2 Emissions (tpy)
Amine Units	0	162
Boilers/heaters/Burners	102	1
Diesel Engines	1,925	92
Drilling Equipment	1,952	238
Flares	46	0.33
Natural Gas Engines	14,938	5
Natural Gas Turbines	2,654	5
Total Emissions (tpy)	21,617	503.33

Table 7-2. Total Non-Platform Emission Estimates.

Source Category	NO$_x$ Emissions (tpy)	SO$_2$ Emissions (tpy)
Drilling Rigs	3,908	659
Helicopters	51	6
Pipelaying Vessels	3,228	542
Platform Construction and Removal Vessels	135	22
Support Vessels	3,275	560
Survey Vessels	4	1
Total OCS Oil/Gas Production Sources (tpy)	10,601	1,790
Commercial Marine Vessels	7,745	1,402
Commercial Fishing Vessels	340	57
Military Vessels	283	60
Total Non-OCS Oil/Gas Production Sources (tpy)	8,368	1,519
Total Non-Platform Emissions (tpy)	18,969	3,309

Table 7-3. Total Platform and Non-Platform Emission Estimates.

Equipment/Source Category	NO$_x$ Emissions (tpy)	SO$_2$ Emissions (tpy)
Total Platform Emissions	21,617	503.33
Drilling Rigs	3,908	659
Helicopters	51	6
Pipelaying Vessels	3,228	542
Platform Construction and Removal Vessels	135	22
Support Vessels	3,275	560
Survey Vessels	4	1
Total OCS Oil/Gas Production Source Emissions	32,218	2,293.33
Total Non-OCS Oil/Gas Production Source Emissions	8,368	1,519
Total Emissions (tpy)	40,586	3,812.33

Table 7-4. Comparison of OCS Platform Emission Estimates.

	Base Year 2000 Inventory	Current Inventory
Total NO_X daily emissions	Minimum: 99 tpd* Maximum: 110 tpd	Average: 59 tpd
Average NO_X daily NGE emissions	90 tpd	40 tpd
Total SO_2 daily emissions	Minimum: 1.1 tpd Maximum: 9.3 tpd	Average: 1.4 tpd
Average SO_2 daily flare emissions	2 tpd	0.001 tpd

* tpd = tons per day

8. REFERENCES

Allison. 2002. Allison Helicopter Engine Manufacturer. Test data for Allison Model 250 helicopter engines.

Boyer, B. and D.K. Brodnax. 1996. Emission Estimation Methods for Oil and Gas Operations. Presented at the Air and Waste Management Association Specialty Conference, The Emission Inventory: Key to Planning, Permits, Compliance, and Reporting. October 4-6, New Orleans, LA.

Brinkman, R. June 19, 2002a. Telephone conversation with Jaime Hauser of Eastern Research Group. U.S. Dept. of the Interior, Minerals Management Service.

Brinkman, R. July 2, 2002b. Email entitled Re: some more on survey vessels, to Jaime Hauser of Eastern Research Group. U.S. Dept. of the Interior, Minerals Management Service.

Coe, D.L., C.A.Gorin, L.R. Chinkin, M. Yocke, and D. Scalfano. 2003. Emission Inventories of OCS Production and Development Activities in the Gulf of Mexico. Final Report. U.S. Department of the Interior, Mineral Management Service, Gulf of Mexico OCS Region, New Orleans, LA. OCS Study MMS 2002-073.

Coe, D.L., D.J. Ladner, J.D. Prouty, L.R. Chinkin, M. Yocke, and D. Scalfano. 2001. User's Guide for the Breton Offshore Activities Data System (BOADS) for Air Quality. Final Report. U.S. Department of the Interior, Minerals Management Service, Gulf of Mexico OCS Region, New Orleans, LA. OCS Study MMS 2000-081.

Cramer, J. June 18, 2001. E-mail entitled Re: fishing locations in the GOM, to Amy Alexander of Eastern Research Group Inc. National Oceanic & Atmospheric Administration.

Dellagiarino, G. June 21, 2001. E-mail entitled Re: more on seismic surveys, to Jaime Hauser of Eastern Research Group Inc. U.S. Dept. of the Interior, Minerals Management Service.

Department of the Navy. 1999. Environmental assessment/overseas environmental assessment of the SH-60R Helicopter/ALFS test program. http://envplan.nfesc.navy.mil/documents/SH60R%20EA.PDF. Accessed October 30, 2001.

EIIP. 1999. Emission Inventory Improvement Program. Volume II. Point Sources. Chapter 10. Oil and Gas Field Production and Processing Operations. http://www.epa.gov/ttn/chief/eiip/techreport/index.html

Froomer, N. May 10, 2002. E-mail entitled 2000 Pipelines, to Richard Billings of Eastern Research Group. U.S. Dept. of the Interior, Minerals Management Service.

Froomer, N. December 9, 2003. E-mail entitled 2001 Pipelines Dataset, to Richard Billings of Eastern Research Group. U.S. Dept. of the Interior, Minerals Management Service.

Helicopter Safety Advisory Conference (HSAC). 2001. Helicopter safety advisory conference (HSAC) Gulf of Mexico offshore helicopter operations and safety review. http://www.hsac.org/stats.html. Accessed October 30, 2001.

Mayes, M. March 14, 2002. E-mail entitled Rig Information, to Roger Chang of Eastern Research Group. Operations Analysis Branch, Minerals Management Service.

McClellan, S. January 9, 2002. Telephone conversation with Roger Chang of Eastern Research Group. USCS Marine Safety Unit, Galveston.

Patella, F. October 22, 2001. E-mail entitled Re: fishing locations in the GOM, to Roger Chang of Eastern Research Group Inc. National Oceanic & Atmospheric Administration.

Peschke, D. May 6, 2002. Facsimile to Roger Chang of Eastern Research Group. Quarter Master, Eighth Coast Guard District, New Orleans, LA.

Poffenberger, J. May 3, 2001. E-mail entitled Re: fishing effort, to Amy Alexander of Eastern Research Group. National Oceanic & Atmospheric Administration.

SCAQMD. 1991. Final Air Quality Management Plan, 1991 Revision, Final Technical Report III-G, 1987 Aircraft Emission Inventory in the South Coast Air Basin.

Thomas, P.F. December 21, 2001. Response to letter from Robert Chang of Eastern Research Group dated December 6, 2001. Commanding Officer USCG Marine Safety Unit, Galveston.

U.S. DOI, Minerals Management Service (MMS). 1995. Gulf of Mexico Air Quality Study: Final Report; Volumes I-III. U.S. Dept. of the Interior, Minerals Management Service, Gulf of Mexico OCS Region, New Orleans, LA. OCS Study MMS 95-0038, 95-0039, and 95-0040.

U.S. DOI, Minerals Management Service (MMS). 2004. Installations, Removals, and Cumulative Totals of Offshore Production Facilities in Federal Waters: 1953-03. http://www.mms.gov/stats/xls(excel)/platformsummary 1942-2003.xls.

U.S. Environmental Protection Agency (EPA). 2002. Compilation of Air Pollutant Emission Factors, Volume I: Stationary Point and Area Sources. *AP-42*. Office of Air Quality Planning and Standards, Research Triangle Park, NC. http://www.epa.gov/ttn/chief/ap42/index.html

U.S. Environmental Protection Agency (EPA). 2003. Documentation for Aircraft, Commercial Marine Vessel, Locomotive, and Other Nonroad Components of the National Emission Inventory. Volume I – Methodology. Emission Factor and Inventory Group, Research Triangle Park, NC. http://www.epa.gov/ttn/chief/net/1999 inventory.html.

U.S. Environmental Protection Agency (EPA). 2000. Analysis of Commercial Marine Vessels Emissions and Fuel Consumption Data. Office of Transportation and Air Quality, Ann Arbor, MI. EPA 420-R-00-002.

U.S. Environmental Protection Agency (EPA). 1992. Procedures for Emission Inventory Preparation, Volume IV: Mobile Sources. Office of Air and Radiation. Ann Arbor, MI. EPA 420-R-92-009.

Wilson D.L., J.N. Fanjoy, and R.S. Billings. 2004. Gulfwide Emission Inventory Study for the Regional Haze and Ozone Modeling Effort: Final Report. U.S. Dept. of the Interior, Minerals Management Service, Gulf of Mexico OCS Region, New Orleans, LA. OCS Study MMS 2004-072.

The Department of the Interior Mission

As the Nation's principal conservation agency, the Department of the Interior has responsibility for most of our nationally owned public lands and natural resources. This includes fostering sound use of our land and water resources; protecting our fish, wildlife, and biological diversity; preserving the environmental and cultural values of our national parks and historical places; and providing for the enjoyment of life through outdoor recreation. The Department assesses our energy and mineral resources and works to ensure that their development is in the best interests of all our people by encouraging stewardship and citizen participation in their care. The Department also has a major responsibility for American Indian reservation communities and for people who live in island territories under U.S. administration.

The Minerals Management Service Mission

As a bureau of the Department of the Interior, the Minerals Management Service's (MMS) primary responsibilities are to manage the mineral resources located on the Nation's Outer Continental Shelf (OCS), collect revenue from the Federal OCS and onshore Federal and Indian lands, and distribute those revenues.

Moreover, in working to meet its responsibilities, the **Offshore Minerals Management Program** administers the OCS competitive leasing program and oversees the safe and environmentally sound exploration and production of our Nation's offshore natural gas, oil and other mineral resources. The MMS **Minerals Revenue Management** meets its responsibilities by ensuring the efficient, timely and accurate collection and disbursement of revenue from mineral leasing and production due to Indian tribes and allottees, States and the U.S. Treasury.

The MMS strives to fulfill its responsibilities through the general guiding principles of: (1) being responsive to the public's concerns and interests by maintaining a dialogue with all potentially affected parties and (2) carrying out its programs with an emphasis on working to enhance the quality of life for all Americans by lending MMS assistance and expertise to economic development and environmental protection.

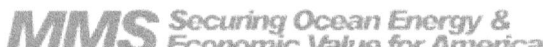